i

Until My Surrender

A Story of Loss, Love and Letting Go

By Shakirah A. Hill

Until My Surrender: A Story of Loss, Love and Letting Go

First published by Shakirah A. Hill
Copyright © 2018 by Shakirah A. Hill

Self-published:hi@shakirahadianna.com

This book is dedicated to Jehovah Rapha—God the Healer. Thank you for keeping every one of your promises. And to my girls: Bako, Candyce, Latoya, Patrice and Teresa. Thank you for being my greatest loves.

iv

TABLE OF CONTENTS

Introduction vii

Part I: This Is My Burden 1

Am I My Mother's Keeper? 3
What's another name for God? 17
Greeted by a Stranger 35
Is This Love? 47

Part II: This is My Surrender 63

Cut To the Bone 65
Dark Night of the Soul 77
Just Before the Dawn 93

Part III: A New Hope 113

Let There Be Light 115
Broken Mirrors and Old Wineskins 133
Food, Forgiveness and the Five Love Languages 145
A New Hope 159
Acknowledgements 168
About the Author 170

Introduction

"Air. I want air, and sunshine, and blue sky, the feeling of the breeze upon my face, the feeling of the turf beneath my feet, and no walls but the far-off mountain tops. Then I am free and strong, once more myself."

- H.W. Longfellow

When I was a little girl I would perch myself near the closest window to stare out into the sky so that I could catch a glimpse of the birds as they migrated. I was envious of their freedom — the way they seemed to move without weight, not eclipsed by any sorrows. As I watched the birds soar out into the great beyond of life, I imagined myself being that unhinged. I imagined being unattached to the realities of my own sense of home.

Growing up in my household was difficult. Pain was an omnipresent and inescapable member of our family. Having a "normal" childhood wasn't something I understood as requisite for becoming a healthily functioning adult but I knew something was amiss when I saw that even birds could be without burden. The birds didn't have to hide behind their wings. They were outstretched, visible, full and ready to move toward whatever was waiting for them. I started to believe this kind of liberty could also be possible for me.

By the time I experienced my first loss at the age of 16, I had learned how to articulate that I wanted more to come from my life than trauma. I wanted to make my pain matter by helping other people who had been hurt like me. I wanted others whose hearts were fragile to know that there was more on the other side of their sadness.

This book is a manifestation of the hope I carried a little more than 16 years ago. I wrote this book because of you. Yes, the story is about me but I wrote it thinking of you, and how it could be in service of finding your own path to letting go.

In the following pages, I share my journey of going from being broken by hardships that were out of my control and enduring heartaches that I walked right into, to being a young woman who understands the value letting go of the past to embrace the grace and mercy of tomorrow — to ultimately knowing that freedom is always within reach. I do not profess to have all the answers or any of the answers for that matter. No story that has been well-lived is tied up with perfect endings and my story is no exemption.

My story does, however, tell the truth of what it means to feel hopeless and without reason. And that with a little bit of faith answers might not come but hope will always follow.

You could say this is a love story, though not the typical love story that ends with a woman and man walking into happily ever after. It's a love story filled with the unexpected revelation that love doesn't always come in the package we desire but the love we are gifted by God (or Allah, or the Universe, or science or serendipity) is always the exact love we need.

You could also say this is a coming of age story. It is a book about finding who you are when there isn't a blueprint for who you're supposed to be and nothing around you provides a template on how to live the kind of life you desire.

However you chose to classify this book — a memoir, a love story, a coming of age tale — I hope that you will see yourself buried in the pages. And as you come out on the other side just as I did, you will outstretch your arms to be seen, visible and full, ready to move toward whatever awaits you.

Before you move on to the first chapter, there are few things worth noting. The first is that I've changed the names of anyone mentioned in this book. As such, I've respected the autonomy of those whose proximity I've benefited from by giving them a pseudonym.

The second thing worth noting is that I am a practicing Christian, in so much as to say that I believe in Jesus, Christ. But this is not a Christian book intended to be a didactic read on how to make your life better by following rules and being religious. The expression of my faith is to illustrate the journey I had to endure to become the person I am intended to be. For me, this meant joining a faith where I could find a value system and a hope that aligned this value system to something greater. I make reference to God as a central character in my life and story. Because I do so, I have chosen to refer to God as *He* and also honor His likeness by capitalizing His name.

If you are not a Christian, I do hope that you will continue reading on. Stories are the great equalizer. We might not believe in the same deity or agree that having a deity is necessary but I can promise you will find something of value in these pages.

Finally, this book was an incredible labor of love. My greatest wish is that you will feel this love in every word, across every chapter on every page.

Now, come with me. Let us let go of everything that entangles us and find our way toward freedom together.

x

Part I: This Is My Burden

Chapter One

Am I My Mother's Keeper?

I slouched in the passenger seat of my mother's car holding my barely showing but swollen abdomen.

"Is it kicking yet?" She asked.

Her voice was stern and steady. My mother spoke deliberately when she stifled her emotions so much so that I could feel the coldness coming from her. I was afraid to tell her that in the exact moment of her asking the baby was, in fact, moving.

At 16-years-old, I was a little more than 20 weeks pregnant and the baby had been moving long since before our car ride headed north of the Beltway. His small kicks felt like flutters of popcorn kernels plucking the inside of my skin, a moment that for any other mother-daughter pair would have been joyous.

But not for us.

My growing belly was a reminder of all the ways the women of the Hill family might come to our demise. Young, black girl carrying the child of a basketball player turned drug dealer. The storyline was so frequent with only a few variations in the details it was difficult to tell who the narrative might have belonged to. My mother? My sister? Me.

The news of my pregnancy, which I hid from my mother as long as I could, was not met with the welcomed anticipation of a grandbaby. Instead, I was given two choices: terminate the pregnancy or find a way to make it on my own.

Up until conceiving my first child, I had managed to keep my adolescent transgressions to a minimum. Aside from normal youthful angst, I was a reasonably mild-mannered child. I excelled academically, often outpacing my peers. I kept a watchful eye on my younger siblings while my mother worked and I stayed in line; trying as best I could not to trigger my mother's temper.

Growing up in my mother's home, our relationship never found its footing even though I remained hopeful someday it would. My mother's abrasiveness and imperviousness was something I had come to accept as part of being the child of an immigrant but it taught me early on that I had to guard myself against the woman who birthed me. The intensity between us was why I didn't tell my mother I was pregnant. It's why I never shared any personal things with her like when I got my first period. That morning I planned to visit my older sister in Crystal City, Va. On the train ride, my stomach repeatedly tensed and pulsed before I felt warm liquid moving down the inner part of my thighs. I didn't know anything about maxi pads or tampons so when I hopped off the train, I ran into department store's bathroom to shove balled up tissue in my panties. Four months after my first period, my mother learned that her daughter was no longer a little girl. We didn't have open conversations. She told me how things were to be and I did my best to tow the line.

Except in the instance when I became with-child.

Despite however cunningly I thought I was hiding being pregnant, my mother was as intuitive. And really, all the signs were there. I went from dancing around the house singing to Destiny's Child on the radio to immediately shutting my bedroom door behind me after school. My boundless energy marked my teenage years - so for me to require so much downtime in my mother's presence, was probably for her, in a word, stunning. Then there was my changing appetite. During the first two months of my pregnancy, I lived on a diet of greens, which wasn't a far cry from what I normally liked to eat, but it was that any other food so desperately repulsed me. While I thought I was being inconspicuous, my mother was quietly adding up all these inconsistencies, arriving at her own summation one evening when I was told to swing by her boyfriend, Jim's house.

I had barely made it through the door before she asked the question I had feared was taking up all the air in the room.

"I'm going to ask you one time and one time only," my mother said. I knew by her tone, the same tone she would later use in the car when she wanted to know if the baby was kicking, that she had realized my greatest secret.

"Are you pregnant?"

"No," I said.

"Shakirah, are you pregnant?"

"No — " My voice weakened and cracked, "I'm not."

I knew it was pointless to continue lying but I was afraid

what might happen if I told the truth. The stillness in the living room made way for the echoing sound of my heart pushing through my chest. Every beat bounced from wall to wall like a pinball until it landed back into my chest. I clenched my fists while my mother and I squared off. If she were going to try and hurt me, I had planned to fight back not for myself but to protect my unborn child. Our silence did not break until my mother walked toward the door to put on her shoes.

"Let's go," she said.

That night my mother arranged an emergency visit to my doctor without my knowledge or consent. In all the time I believed to have been concealing my pregnancy, my mother was making her own plans. It seems that if I were not going to tell her the truth she would devise a way to find out on her own. As we sat in the waiting room of Dr. Kay's office, I tried to quickly think of how I could avoid answering any questions about my pregnancy. Dr. Kay had been my pediatrician since my mother, brother and I moved to Maryland from New York. Though I didn't know her outside of her medical practice, I felt safe when speaking with her. Dr. Kay had a warmth that I didn't encounter often. I foolishly believed that whatever was to happen in the examination room, Dr. Kay and I could keep between us.

"Shakirah..." Dr. Kay's assistant called out from behind the glass partition of the waiting room. "Shakirah Hill?"

"Yes, that's me."

"Dr. Kay is ready to see you."

Before I walked back into the room where all my secrets would unravel before me like a ball of ill-kept yarn, my mother, who was remaining in the waiting room, and I exchanged glances. To me, all I saw was a disheartened and deeply disappointed mother looking toward her lonely and misunderstood child.

"Shakirah, do you know why you're here?" Dr. Kay asked me as I made my way toward the examination table.

"Not really," I said.

The room was cool yet heat filled my body as Dr. Kay looked intently in my direction. It was as though everyone could see through every layer of me to my secret, the one I thought up until now, I had been keeping so well.

"Okay — would it be alright if I checked out a few things? Your mother has some concerns about you and I want to assure her that you're fine"

"Sure, that's no problem, Dr. Kay," I said.

"Great. I'm going to step out so you can change into the robe over there."

I draped the ash blue medical gown over my petite frame that Dr. Kay left for me on the examination table. When she came back and found me swaddled in the polyester gown, she started the examination by checking my heart rate.

"Don't worry, Shakirah. Everything is going to be okay." She assured me after noticing my increasing heart rate.

"Your heart rate is a little fast but your blood pressure looks good. Now if you could just lie back, I want to check a few more things."

Dr. Kay began asking about my period and sexual history. She wanted to know when I had my last period and if I was sexually active? I couldn't remember the date of my last period, which I offered as an answer and I was adamant that I was, under no circumstances, pregnant. She asked if I was sure. Yes, I was sure. I said. I clung to the lie as if my life depended on it. Dr. Kay ran her hands over my abdomen and gently pressed.

"Do you feel that?"

Am I My Mother's Keeper?

"Yes," I responded, letting tears I had been holding back for months begin rolling down my cheeks.

"Can you put your feet in the stirrups for me?" Dr. Kay asked.

Not long after following Dr. Kay's instruction I felt pressure coming from the inside of me. This was not the same sensation or popcorn-like fluttering I had come to know as my child. It was, I suspected, Dr. Kay's fingers touching the outside of my uterus gently coming into proximity with the lie I had been repeating to myself day after day for five months. Dr. Kay's round blue eyes softened as the pulled her fingers away from my body. The baby moved as if trying not to make himself known. I sat upright on the table, trying not to let my mother hear my sobs. My secret had been shared before I was ready. Without a plan, I felt hopeless. Dr. Kay asked how long I knew I was pregnant. She told me that because I was a minor she would have to tell my mother of the pregnancy. The doctor went to the waiting room to share the news. I sat back in the examination room trying to regain my breath, to find my footing and possibly an exit from which to run.

On the car ride back from Dr. Kay's office my mother presented my options. She told me that she would not raise another child in her household and that if I decided to keep the baby I was no longer welcome under her roof. Before that evening I didn't want to think of a plan beyond the following day and there my mother was telling me to decide my child's fate. I didn't feel confident that I could make it out on the streets with a child alone. My natural response was what it had always been – to fall in line with whatever it was my mother demanded and be mindful not to further agitate her frustrations.

It was certain, as her threats and name calling reverberated to my bones, that I would be hard-pressed to find another option at that moment. My body, now added to the list of betrayals I had already endured.

"What's it going to be?" she screamed. "What are you going to do, Shakirah?"

My mother and I sat divided between her hostility and my fear. We were both afraid. I didn't know what my child's life would become growing up in the same environment where I had inherited anxiety, shame, and latent depression. It was clear that my mother was terrified a child would hold me back perhaps in the ways she felt held back from pursuing her dreams.

I was her mirror, one she helped to keep unblemished and from repeating the same indiscretions she committed in her youth. Though my mother lacked the ability to express her deepest desires and love for me, under the guise of her frustrated bellicose was a woman who wanted her daughter to win. It wasn't until years later that I would gain the insight that parents can only work with the tools they have been given. My mother's love was not soft or gentle. She did not bake cookies and read bedtime stories. All she knew to do was try with all her might to protect her children even when her protection would bring its own degrees of pain. The morning following my visit to Dr. Kay's office my mother scheduled a second-trimester pregnancy termination.

***

The story of Patsy and my dysfunction begins in the countryside of St. Elizabeth, one of Jamaica's largest parishes. It was in St. Elizabeth, between the harshness of Jamaica's ghettos and the beauty of the mountains, my mother became the daughter of a Cuban-born entrepreneurial woman and fiercely rugged Jamaican man.

My grandmother's success as a business owner allowed

her to move Patsy from Jamaica to England where she would spend her formative years. Being schooled in some of England's most prestigious boarding schools allowed Patsy to discover her love of the performing and fine arts. It didn't take long for Patsy to learn that her lean body and instinctive poise was made for ballet. Patsy spent weekdays dancing and the weekends working for her mother at a bed and breakfast. Patsy was my grandmother's only child but their story was also precarious. My grandmother placed high expectations on her daughter exacting that Patsy would be the crowning jewel of all her achievements. In this way, Patsy and I were one in the same. We were both young women desperately wanting to live up to our mother's ideals.

When I consider what might have been the point in my mother's life that led her to become the emotionally distant and cold woman I came to know, I suspect it begins with the slow sensation of one too many passes of gin hitting the throat. I imagine it was watching her father drink bottle after bottle after bottle of the devil's juice. And then bearing witness to his evolution from father to monster.

My grandmother was often too harsh with my mother but it was my grandfather's alcoholism that truly broke Patsy's heart. His drinking problem was so severe that long after my grandfather passed away, Patsy would say she could often still smell the stench of gin in the air. Though he was deceased, my grandfather never truly left my mother. His presence always tormented her in the most insidious of ways.

My grandfather's absenteeism baited my mother into the arms of men who repeated the same pattern of abuse she experienced from her father. Every kick, punch, and slap Patsy dolled out to my siblings and me were sparked from the decades of bruises she sustained at the hands of her drunken father. Often as an insult, Patsy would angrily say, "You are just like your father," which was to suggest that I was no good, just like him. And in those moments I wondered if she was less upset with me and more repulsed by the idea that she might be just like *her* father. Perhaps it was that my desire to be a child reminded her of all the ways she couldn't and so I couldn't be like my father because she did not want to be like hers.

My grandfather was always there; always perched on my mother's shoulders like a puppet master pulling her strings and whispering in her ear, *you are worthless.* She would repeat those words to me not knowing she was being controlled by a haunting distant past and with every word, with every aggression together, we would become worthless and broken.

***

Our car ride north of the Beltway would lead to one of the few clinics in New York City that performed late trimester pregnancy terminations. I knew better than to ask Patsy any questions about what was going to happen once we arrived. Instead, I allowed the quiet tension of our trip to be my comfort. The journey back to the city where I was birthed would be where I would end my child's life. If those 600 miles were going to be the last moments I could spend with my baby, I wanted them for myself.

To an outsider, the presence of my young, lithe body hunched over in the waiting room chair while picking away at my fingernails was the result of my decisions. I certainly thought so. Back then I believed that I was the first one to knock over the domino that became the catalyst for a turn of events that led me to that waiting room on a very cold January day in New York. But the pieces had begun falling long before the waiting room, long before that night I lost

Am I My Mother's Keeper?

my virginity at age 15 and long before I entered the world. In time I would learn that I did not knock over the first domino. Rather, I was caught in a generational tailspin, and this trip to the waiting room was par for the course.

Looking around the waiting area of the clinic I noticed the other women carrying their own burdens and decisions. Some of the women looked anxious, messing with their hair and flicking their pens repeatedly. That made me wonder if I appeared anxious, too. My leg was shaking, which may have made my nervousness obvious. Sitting among those women, it was clear that all attempts at normalcy had escaped me.

After a quick glance around the facility, I immediately knew everyone's tick; I was the eponymous leg shaker. The small-framed yet stern-faced woman seated across from me sifted through her paperwork, wrote frantically, placed it in a neat pile and then shuffled through her papers once more. The woman seated to the left of me didn't even bother filling out her questionnaire, though we were all expected to before we could be taken into the next room. She just stared blankly at the signage on the parallel wall. I could tell that her eyes weren't following the emergency instructions on the poster.

Though I didn't fully understand the nuance of the termination and all the ways I would be impacted following my abortion, I knew that what was going to happen in the next room would further breach my mother and me. Somehow in my young mind, I was well aware that the stance she had taken would erode any opportunity for me to fully trust her.

Unlike myself and the other women in the clinic, my mother was impervious. This wasn't surprising, as she was never one to emote. Even if something were bothering her down to the pit of her soul, my mother would let those emotions bypass like a stranger on the street. *You have no business here. Keep it moving,* is what I imagined she told her feelings when they invited themselves into her heart. I often wondered if she was born that way, or if life knocked her around so much that hardness became her only method of survival. Whatever the case, she sat in the waiting room unmoved by the clock that seemed to tick louder and louder as each minute passed, or by the woman who was frazzled by all of the paperwork. My leg shaking was of no consequence to my mother.

"Sha-kiy-irah?" a woman with a deep, New York accent called out.

I had grown accustomed to people placing added emphasis on the wrong syllables in my name – always drawing out on the "kee" too much, but never enough on the "rah."

The nurse who would assist the doctor with my pregnancy termination had an eerily sunny disposition. I assumed it was protocol to be detached in order to make the work more manageable. I barely wanted to be there as the patient and gathered it was no walk in the park for her either. After all, she would probably see hundreds of girls and women like me. The detachment had to be the only logical way to survive in her profession. At least that's what I told myself to avoid from crying as she handed me a hospital gown and provided clear directions on how the procedure would work: I would be given anesthesia, and then I would count backward from 10 until I fell asleep. By the time I woke up the procedure would be complete, and I would no longer be pregnant. As she said those words, "no longer pregnant," a jolting pang rang through the pit of my stomach. It was as if the baby knew too that our time together was coming to an end. The nurse assured me that the procedure would be painless; there would only be mild discomfort in the post-op. I would soon learn that there would, in fact, be pain, and the discomfort would last much longer than expected.

The doctor entered the room less cheery than my nurse.

"Young lady, do you understand what you're about to do?" He asked while placing his hand on my shoulder, offering the standard procedural compassion.

"Yes," I said tersely, not wanting to go any further into the conversation.

"Alright," he said. "Let's have you lie back so we can get started." The doctor and nurse stood over me and coached me as I began to count.

"Ten..." My eyes felt heavy, blinking slowly. "Nine..." I saw a flash of light. "Eight..." I thought I heard a voice, but I wasn't sure if it was the nurse, the doctor, or my own mind telling me, "*You're going to be okay.*"

The numbness caused by the anesthesia prohibited me from feeling anything but the wetting of tears moistening the side of my face. The nurse and doctor started moving in slow motion. For a moment it was like a nightmare. Before I could jump off the operating table and escape with my child, everything faded to black...

***

I woke up in a room that looked like a war-zone hospital filled with wounded soldiers. Women on stretchers lay moaning in agony. My memory was still groggy from the anesthesia, and for a moment I couldn't recall where I was or why I was there. As I came to my senses, I immediately ran my hands over my stomach. Empty. Another nurse, also eerily cheerful, walked around handing out pamphlets with information on support groups we could attend. Still holding my lifeless belly, I reached for the pamphlets only to appease the nurse. Once her back was turned I dropped them on the stretcher and made my way to the waiting room. Every trace of what had just happened was to be left behind. I didn't want to sit in a support group reliving the details of the day. I didn't want to talk about my feelings. I just wanted to go home.

Following my abortion, my mother became even more adamant about me keeping up with school the way I had previously done. No concessions were made for falling behind, which wasn't problematic for me. I loved school; it was my escape from the craziness of everyday life. In school, I found a confidence that I could not find at home, which made me one of the few students who wanted to be in class each day. Even more so, finding normalcy was critical once I returned.

On my first day back I spotted my best friend. We didn't talk about what happened. Instead, the moment I entered the lunchroom he gave me one of those hugs you don't know you need until you find yourself nestled in the embrace. I masked my tears behind half-hearted jokes about him smelling like old cafeteria food. Then we went on as if our worlds hadn't been changed by my indiscretion. I struggled with reconciling what I had done in hopes of preserving my future. I wanted to be successful, to be different from my family, but I felt so undeserving since my pregnancy termination. To find what I believed to be peace in the midst of my internal turmoil, I often spoke to my baby at night before bed. I named him Jabari, meaning brave. I told him that I would not allow the ending of his life to be in vain and that I would make something of myself. I would be the kind of woman he would have been proud to have as his mother. No one knew that under my pillow I kept the sonogram taken just before my abortion. I wanted to hold on to him for as long as I could, even if only in the smallest way.

The remainder of my sophomore year passed quickly. It didn't take long for me to begin immersing myself into my schoolwork. I enlisted into AP classes that would allow me to receive college credits if I passed the AP tests. With my mother's reluctant permission, I even started participating in dance and drama activities again. The memory of the abortion clinic was starting to fade behind me. All the work I did to hide my deepest regret seemed to be paying off. I still struggled at night with tears greeting me just as my head hit the pillow, but my conversations with Jabari were becoming less frequent.

The less I thought and spoke of my unborn baby, the easier it was for me to ignore what had happened. My relationship with my mother was no better than before, but I didn't care. From the moment she left me with the decision to abort my child or find my own way, a line had been drawn. Whatever admiration I had for her dissipated. I wanted to forge a new path — my own path. And the first step was admitting that I wasn't going to be like her.

But maybe I already was?

***

Chapter Two

What's another name for God?

Just as the trees and flowers rise up to meet spring, I was also beginning to reemerge. The small, barely noticeable bump that had enlarged my abdomen was completely gone by the time the last quarter of school came around. Only minor remnants of my pregnancy remained. The breast milk my body produced slowly evaporated or, on rare occasion, leaked when I was near a crying infant. The fullness of my cheeks had become slimmer but not too much. The youthful roundness of my face was still there to remind me that even though I had carried a child I was just a teenage girl who had gotten herself into an adult situation. Watching my frame change back to its original petite, lithely form was like watching the last bit of snow melt away after a long and harsh winter. And seamlessly falling asleep at night was also a gradual progression.

But it wouldn't be long before the ghost of pain would haunt me again.

Patsy and I continued circling one another like a predator and its prey. We never spoke about what happened in the abortion clinic or how the pregnancy termination impacted me. Instead, we moved about life as we had come to define "normal." Though I lacked the agency to articulate how disappointed I was in my mother's response to my pregnancy and her lack of compassion thereafter, I became even more determined to build a life outside of her household. A quiet rebellion had been stewing inside me. I was determined to leave — to slip away like the first drops of rain that speckle windows.

My naivete emboldened and betrayed me. What I couldn't see were the ways Patsy tried to manage her own pain: retreating to her boyfriend's house with every opportunity she could find to ignore the problems that had confronted our family. She was a woman acting out of fear, a woman who hadn't learned to package her love with softness and who hadn't learned to accept the love of her children, a love that was sometimes messy and misguided, but love, nonetheless.

My mother's expectation of my school performance never wavered and was a welcomed gift that would set my life on an upward trajectory. The environment at home was erratic but walking through the doors of Eastern was like entering a hidden world.

Each day I traversed through the dilapidated hallways. The ceilings hung so low that every guy at school could reimagine himself as much taller than he actually was. There were more than 1500 students at Eastern and it was obvious given the amount of noise that rumbled through the school's corridors. Though the student population was predominantly minority, we were still largely segregated.

Yo! Tomaré tu almuerzo!

Hombre cállate y toma estas nueces—

The crew from El Salvador congregated in the courtyard of the cafe comforted by the security of the unity of a shared language and shared immigrant experiences. There were speculations that some of the guys were members of gangs, which made them largely untouchable. Slightly south of the courtyard nestled a raggedy basketball court displaying only one hoop with torn netting at the brim. The Black guys from each of the sports departments occupied the four corners of the blacktop. Fights breaking out on the court were a common occurrence.

Tell that nigga I'll slap the taste out his mouth if he comes over here again —

Dawg, fuck that shit. Fuck that nigga ... catch that nigga on the avenue.

The line between the seriousness and jovialness of these brawls was a finely drawn strait. Inevitably, an administrator would be overheard calling for reinforcement to break up the fights but not without having to break through a crowd of students instigating the fight to go further.

Back inside, scattered across the cafe, were the rest of us who were not separated by our ethnicity, but by our interests. Seated together and made noticeable by donning the latest trends and most pristine sneakers were the popular kids whose parents had the means to provide their children with allowances and plump bank accounts. Ruckus could be heard from the tables in the back of the cafe where the Black nerds swapped Pokemon trading cards and gossiped over anime plotlines.

While the El Salvadorians and athletes took over the courtyard and the well-dressed popular kids cracked jokes about those whose sartorial choices were beneath them, I

What's another name for God?

was in the library discovering worlds outside Brooklyn and the country we moved to follow our family's voyage down the Mid-Atlantic.

"Ms. Hill, you need to remember to logout of the computer before going to your next class, understand?"

The school librarians knew me by name and if a lunch hour passed without me making a pit stop into the library, they would send hall monitors to come to look for me. During the few months that I was pregnant, the school library was a retreat. I would grab a salad from the cafe and nestle in between the columns of bookshelves. My first trimester forced me into an occasional nap. Between the works of Richard Wright and Toni Morrison, I would place my back against the old dusty shelves. With my knees folded into my baby bump, my head would flop down on top my chest. Before I could catch myself I would be off into a dream.

School was where I could be the most authentic version of myself and it was where I was permitted to be a teenager. My teachers were compassionate, dedicated mentors. In chemistry, Mr. Dieterle taught us about chemical bonding and elemental structures while being a listening ear for whatever adolescent issues my peers and I brought into his classroom.

Mrs. Vogel, the school's AP Psychology teacher, used every Friday to form a "safety circle" to make help us apply the psychological theories we learned about each week to what we were experiencing in our own lives: at home, in school, and internally. Mrs. Vogel class is where I first learned to be reflective and introspective about the trauma I had been experiencing. I never used the word trauma and really didn't see my experience as particularly abnormal because at my high school of my peers were facing many of the same problems I was dealing with. Few people knew I got pregnant and subsequently terminated the pregnancy but had the news circulated more broadly, it wouldn't have been a shocking revelation. The year I got pregnant at least four other girls in my graduating class had gotten pregnant, too. Most of the students were being raised by single mothers and more than half of the student population was from lower-income neighborhoods. We were overlooked, misunderstood and forgotten about in the larger societal discourse.

But school was our solace. It was my solace.

And it was in that school where I would meet my first husband, Kyle. Kyle was the quiet type. The kind of guy who walked through the halls as if he remained perpetually suspicious of his surroundings while also being open to the possibility of a new friend, a new encounter. He was always a bit contradictory. We were a year apart and hadn't crossed paths until I was moved from junior English to Mrs. Vogel's class. Because he had strategically positioned himself in the back of the classroom he was easy to miss. The only moments that anyone ever remembered he was enrolled in the class was when he would respond to other student's questions posed to Mrs. Vogel with snarky quips. Each time it would be the same. Someone would raise their hand to ask Mrs. Vogel a question about homework or a research study of psychological antiquity and then Kyle would jump in.

"You would know the answer to that if you read the homework," he would say.

Rarely did anyone defends themselves against Kyle. A few students would tell him to shut up or toss a crumpled sheet of paper his way. But no one had ever challenged him.

What an asshole. I would think to myself. But I never looked back until the day I overheard Kyle making a comment to Julissa, one of the El Salvadorian girls from the courtyard.

What's another name for God?

"...Her father probably sells oranges on the street," Kyle whispered to Derek who was sitting at the desk next to him.

"You foul man," Derek said before letting out a half-hearted laugh.

"That's not funny," I said turning towards Kyle.

Kyle was leaned back in his chair as if pleased with his insult. Our eyes remained locked without either of us offering further commentary.

"I was joking," he quipped.

"It wasn't funny. You don't know her or her family."

Kyle pulled himself up to his desk crossing his arms across the surface. For the first time, I could see him — truly see him. Kyle boasted broad shoulders and full, muscular arms that made his body appear too mature for his age. He was kind on the eyes; with a caramel complexion and pronounced cheekbones that would make a supermodel envious. His partially wavy and moderately kinky hair was corn rolled straight back, a style most of the guys were wearing in the early 2000s. It came as no surprise that Kyle played football. He was Eastern's first-string wide-receiver and the best friend of the school's quarterback, Mario.

"And Shakirah, who was it that trained his dog to salivate at the sound of a dinner bell?" Mrs. Vogel asked, bringing my attention back to the lesson.

I cut my eyes at Kyle once more before responding. "Pavlov."

Since our brief encounter during Mrs. Vogel's class, I would notice Kyle walking the hallways or see him across the courtyard with the other athletes. We didn't speak following the previous incident until the computer I was using in the small computer lab at the back of Mrs. Vogel's class broke. Kyle, who was seated next to me, offered a few suggestions for getting the computer to work again. There were moments when Kyle could be kind — gentle even. That day as we sat at the computers skimming Black Planet, we exchanged a few laughs, a few glimpses and an agreement to be agreeable.

From the computer lab, Kyle would begin meeting me at my locker to walk me to class and soon he would walk me home after school. Our walks turned into long phone conversations that I would hide from Patsy. In the months that I learned more about Kyle, I saw that our worlds were completely different but in many ways the same. We were both products of single mother households, though Kyle's relationship with his mother was much more tender and secure than mine. Kyle's family lived in a single family house in a relatively nice neighborhood. His mother, a minister, had been able to support her four sons on a sizable government salary offering the family a kind of security I would not come to know until adulthood.

The clear and crisp spring sky began giving way to the haziness of an early summer. Summers in the Mid-Atlantic always brought an added bit of moisture in the air. The school days were getting shorter and Kyle was preparing for graduation. I was becoming a rising senior and setting my sights on college. Kyle and I had never explicitly defined our friendship. We were spending a great deal of time together and I suspected that he liked me. It would be one phone call on a Saturday afternoon following the Hill family ritual of a weekly household deep cleaning that the trajectory of our lives would change.

"Why do you expect that I would come visit you when I'm away at college?" Kyle asked me.

"What do you mean?"

"Like, why would I come see you? What would motivate me to come home for you?" He followed up. For a moment

What's another name for God?

I considered that all the time we were spending together was deeper than friendship and though we had not come to a mutual agreement on the nature of our friendship I believed we were a couple.

"Because you're my boyfriend," I said.

"I am?" Kyle responded, sounding confused.

"Yeah – you're my boyfriend. That should be your motivation to come visit me."

"And when did I become your boyfriend?"

"Do you not want to be?" I asked.

"I'll be your boyfriend," Kyle said. This was the conversation — a conversation devoid of intentionality and direction — that would lead us into almost a decade-long relationship.

Those three words, "You're my boyfriend" would propel us towards a path that led to a broken marriage and ultimately divorce. But first, on a sunny and hot Saturday afternoon, we would start our journey as two young lovers.

I didn't want Kyle to know me—not the real me—so, I hid behind good grades and bold aspirations as a decoy. In our young relationship, I shared more about what life would be like for me someday than what life was truly like. At any moment I could be found talking his head off about the future, my future. And Kyle would sit quietly waiting for me to finish rattling off my ambitions.

Kyle didn't seem to mind the illusion. In fact, I think he preferred keeping our dating superficial because superficiality meant he didn't have to shoulder the weight of my emotions. On the rare occasions when my guard slipped and my skeletons were visible, Kyle grew uneasy in my presence. "Why do things have to be so heavy?" he would say when I couldn't hold back the darkness of latent depression. Then, I would realize my mask had fallen off forcing me to find a way to get us back to the shore again. My waters were treacherous. And it was clear Kyle wasn't ready for the waves.

There were many things that made me fall for Kyle, like how easy it was to get lost in the richness of his brown, almond-shaped eyes. Or, how his pensiveness made him appear more mature than his age. Even though I detested his sarcastic humor—which was often targeted at me—I adored the way he worked up his whole body to laugh. I liked Kyle for the superficial reasons a teenage girl likes a guy, but nothing rivaled what his presence meant to me.

What he lacked in emotional generosity Kyle made up for in consistency. Even if Kyle was making jokes about me he did so while talking to me on the phone each night, or on our daily walks to my locker. Our weekend retreats away from school work, and my family drama made me feel like someone who mattered—even if only a little bit. It was ironic that Kyle hadn't done anything particularly heroic to win my affections. I could sense that he wasn't overwhelmed with admiration for me. But, his constant physical presence was sufficient enough to keep my heart. When I needed him he was there, and his being there was all I needed.

***

The first time I began understanding different family dynamics other than my own was when I began meeting Kyle's family. This was also my first true exposure to Christianity.

I met Kyle's mother at our school's fall opening track meet during Kyle's senior year. Kyle had asked me during our walk to my locker in between classes if I planned to come to the meet. My dance team was on a brief hiatus, so I had the time to spare.

"I'll be on the bleachers by 4:30. My mom will be there, too." Kyle said as I placed my calculus books on the top shelf of my locker. "Just meet us there."

"Okay," I responded.

Being introduced to Kyle's mother didn't strike me as a monumental to our dating. I didn't see our meeting like how it often happened in movies where the narrative of two young lovers suddenly grew more interesting because the families had come into the scene. I was just curious where Kyle had inherited his eyes and what about his family made him so quiet, so reflective. After five months of dating, we hadn't talked much about our families. I had my own reasons, but Kyle seemed like the kind of guy who came from a normal, loving family. If nothing else, meeting his mom seemed seemed like it could help me understand Kyle more. I wasn't looking for anything else outside of that.

"Oh," he said turning back to me as he headed towards his next class. "When you meet my mom don't curse. She's a pastor."

Kyle's mother was a minister at a small community church where Kyle spent his childhood learning to recite scripture, pray and understand the foundation of civility. Kyle's mother was a petite woman whose body size in no way took away from the dynamism of her presence. I had met very few pastors before, yet when I met Kyle's mother for the first time, I could tell she was different.

I did as Kyle instructed and met him and his mother on the bleachers at 4:30. He made introductions just before heading to the track to prepare for his meet.

"Ma, this is Shakirah...Shakirah, this is my mom."

"Hi," I said while trying to hide the anxiety that had overtaken me.

Kyle's mom gave me a glance and smiled. We stood side-by-side watching Kyle stretch at the starting line.

"Is this your first time seeing Ky run?" She asked.

"Yes, I'm usually in dance practice during the meets, but I'm excited I finally get to catch a race."

"Now, Shakirah does your name mean anything?"

"Oh, it's Arabic. It means grateful."

"Shakirah...that's pretty."

The runners assumed the starting position just before the race gun went off. A loud bang echoed in the air and the crowd started to scream, cheering on each of the runners. I turned to my left to find Kyle's mom was cheering, too. Kyle was different on the track. He moved swiftly past the other runners. There was an intensity I hadn't seen in him before. The faster he moved the louder I screamed. Nothing was holding him back. He was free. I wanted him to win. I wanted that for me, too.

Mom, as she told me to call her, walked like she had an entourage of angels surrounding her. There was a confidence in the way she carried herself; her head always held high and her shoulders at ease. Her self-assurance made it easy for me to gravitate toward her. At times I forgot Mom was a devoted woman of the cloth because when the idea of a minister came to mind, I wouldn't have pictured Kyle's mother. In fact, I had always assumed ministers were slick-talking older men who wore bad suits and made every effort to con people into heaven. Mom was the opposite. Her southern colloquialisms were always parable-like, filled with gems of wisdom. Mom had all boys, Kyle being her youngest and favorite. She knew Kyle like the lyrics of her favorite hymn. Of all her songs, he was her favorite note to sing and their bond was deep. I appreciated she would be so willing to extend that same warmth to me.

What's another name for God?

What I knew of faith in my family was that we were not a particularly religious group. There were small dalliances of spirituality from my childhood. Though my mother was raised Catholic, my parents fell in love as young Rastafarians, not relegated to the dogma of traditional religion. I inherited their amorphous approach to faith. If you asked me then whether or not I believed in God, specifically the Christian God, I would have said that if there was a God, that there are many avenues to find Him or Her. I would have told you that religion is dangerous and we should be careful not to believe anything we cannot prove. I grew up in a family that walked by survival and not faith. We did not put out hope in a God in the sky but in sheer will, a solid work ethic, and the accessibility that a good education permits.

We didn't go to church on Sunday; opposite of what I noticed was standard in Maryland—a state that carries remnants of the Bible Belt. The concept of the Christian God was introduced to me by one of my first friends in Maryland who told me her grandmother prayed to Him regularly. She invited me to attend a few church services which my mother permitted. I suspect she felt church was one of the few safe spaces where I could exert some form of youthful autonomy, except that I found the experience to be empty and baseless.

When Kyle invited me to attend his church, he never explicitly asked about my religious beliefs. I suspect that given what he knew of my family history and my pregnancy termination he might have believed I needed a savior. If saving me was his intention then he wasn't too far off the mark. I did need saving, but I wasn't ready to open myself up to the reality of what it would take to be saved. Kyle's invitation was not met with warm receptivity, but because I enjoyed the dynamic of his family, I went along every so often.

When I attended school I sat in the front row, not to appease my teachers, but sitting in the front made me feel as though I were taking in knowledge by way of osmosis. I wanted a fresh anointing of what I was learning. My approach to church going with Kyle was the opposite. I made sure we sat in the back, or off to the side in the event I needed to make a quick escape. Sitting in the back gave me the vantage point of watching everyone else. I still remember the sound of the organ playing as old women with flamboyant headdresses swayed to the steady sound of the organ keys. They clenched church programs with the lyrics to hymnals from antiquity in their wrinkled hands while their brown faces glistened from the heat. I kept watching, mouthing the lyrics as if I knew what I was singing. *We've come this far by faith*...I could see some of the women's body developing a slight bounce. Their feet lifted off the floor as shouts echoed through the room. Hallelujahs encouraged the organist to pick up the tempo. *Leaning on the Lord*...Kyle rocked back and forth to the music, clapping to the beat. I was impressed he knew all the songs without reading the program.

Mom was always in the front row. Sometimes she bounced too, jumping in circles with her hands crossing from her hips to slightly above her stomach. And there was always one person who was guaranteed to pass out. No one was moved when this happened, maybe because it occurred regularly. They would place a white cloth over them and the church service continued. They were entranced at the music, moved by something larger, or the heat that filled the small sanctuary. Once I asked Kyle what was happening and he said that a person who had fallen out "caught the Spirit." It was weird and I wanted to leave before this Spirit came looking for me.

Pastor Elliott, a heavy-set black man with a deep southern drawl carried a cane as he limped to the pulpit. He stood before the congregation equipped with two things: a

What's another name for God?

handkerchief in the breast pocket of his shirt and a word from God. Beads of sweat framed his forehead while he spoke on the goodness of God and the inherent folly of humanity. Sin was a popular topic for these sermons. I wondered if the pastor, who could hear from God, knew about my abortion. I wondered if he could smell the sin on me like spoiled milk.

I grew accustomed to the ceremony of service as I continued attending the small community church with Kyle and his mother. The elderly women began learning my name and giving me acknowledging glances when I walked through the church doors. Sometimes the glances were followed by whispers to seatmates. Kyle's ex-girlfriend was known for attending service with him, too. Being the replacement had its drawbacks. Still, I worked diligently to ensure Kyle and Mom's legacy remained untarnished. Without being raised Christian, I understood the politics of going to church. Each Sunday I bowed my head in prayer, conforming to the ritual—the hands raised, the falling praise from wretched sinners with hopes of being thought a good Christian girl honorable enough for the minister's son lest anyone discover me—the real me.

In certain services, people share their story, during what was called their testimony. These testimonies usually started with how difficult life was before God came along. And the testimonies always ended with God miraculously turning their lives around. Miracles! God was working miracles, they would say. Babies born to barren parents. Employment where there had been no sight of job prospects. Once loveless marriages reinvigorated with affection. The stories were ripe with God's alleged kindness. Fellow congregation members shouted in agreement when the person sharing their testimony would say, "But God." The organ player would hit the same three keys and the whole sanctuary would erupt. Kyle watched the spectacle with the same countenance of a stenographer, taking note of the speaker and their words with careful regard. He knew these people, their lives—what they overcame and yet I could sense he remained unmoved by what was supposed to be a powerful demonstration of God. I maintained curiosity with each testimony.

One Sunday Pastor Elliott asked the congregation a pointed question.

"Church —" he said with his deep voice blaring through the faulty sound system. "What's another name for God?"

The fan hissed over the sound of men and women looking around for a hint of where the sermon might be headed. "Let me put it another way," Pastor Elliott refrained.

"When we're in trouble, what do we call God?"

Helper.

Healer.

Provider.

Sustainer.

Voices sprung up throughout the service like Whack-a-mole. I felt like I might be the only person not following the pastor's line of logic.

"He is all those things, church. And more." Pastor Elliott continued, "When Moses asked God who should he tell the Israelites that God is, God, replied tell them that I AM." Pastor Elliott explained that God referred to himself open-endedly to account for His vastness and that because God is vast, His power is limitless.

"There is nothing God cannot do because He is I AM. This is God's name."

I was offended at the assertion because while for some that might have felt true, I had been attending church regularly and my life was the same. My mother and I were still at odds. The loneliness still pursued me in my quiet moments and I was still harboring my dark secret. Either God's miracles were only reserved for special people or He was a fraud. Of course, I was happy to acknowledge God as existing in some capacity, whether in the sky or in the imagination of the believer. I even had to give credit to His vivid imagination in creating the earth. But, the theory the pastor and naïve churchgoers were peddling about God being all-powerful and in control of our lives struck me as unfounded. My life was out of control and to make sense of it, I was doing all the work. Whatever miracles occurring in my life would come from me, not some God in the sky.

***

Nothing was coming of our church attendance accept routine. It was obvious Kyle didn't understand me. He didn't know that backing out of plans or brushing me off was eroding my capacity to trust. He also didn't care much for my family history and remained surface level about his. And honestly, I didn't understand him. I filtered our young relationship through the lens of my pain. I couldn't see Kyle as a young adult male who was ignorant about what he had taken on in dating me. I wanted to be loved deeply, to find my home in the heart of someone. I wanted safety and consistency. I wanted assurance my life wouldn't continue to be a series of unfortunate events. Kyle wasn't originally part of the plan I created, but the more we dated the more I found a place for him. I began writing him in my story as a leading character. Kyle rarely expressed his emotions, making it difficult to know if his feelings ran as deep as mine. There were spaces of Kyle's mind I couldn't reach, but he kept showing up day-after-day and that was enough for me.

After one service Kyle mentioned Pastor Elliott was his Godfather and a paternal figure in his life. I wasn't a fan of going to church but I knew the emptiness of not having my real father around so I supported Kyle having someone to fill the space. In passing, Kyle mentioned his father, a few times he called Mom's house to speak to his older brother Jonathan. Kyle answered the phone, but his father didn't seem to care. "He never wants to speak to me," he said. "He only asks for Jonathan." It was one of the few times I could see the pain in Kyle. I was well versed in the expression of agony and when Kyle passed along the call to Jonathan I saw it in his face. I knew it was haunting him in the quiet, but it would be another issue we wouldn't talk about.

***

What's another name for God?

Chapter Three

Greeted by a Stranger

More than a decade of time lapsed between my Winston and me but the events of his return happened quickly. An exchange of phone calls between my parents initiated by an aunt in Jamaica led my mother to send my father pictures of me.

She's beautiful, Winston told Patsy during one of their conversations.

My mother mentioned to my father that my high school graduation was quickly approaching and that she felt strongly that his presence would be a welcomed addition. "Before you know it she'll be a grown woman," my mother said during a phone call with Winston I overheard. She spoke of Kyle and that when my father planned to visit, Kyle's house is where he could find me. There was an exchange of phone numbers —Patsy's delicate penmanship inscribed my father's number on a torn sheet of paper. I glimpsed at the paper with the perfectly penned number realizing that the only thing standing between my father and me was ten numbers. My nervousness hindered me from picking up the phone and calling. Winston was still so far but yet drawing close.

At the sound of his voice during our first call since the last time we had seen each other a decade prior, I spiraled back into childhood. Winston spoke as if we were never estranged. He sounded like a man who had been collecting memories and stories with his daughter. Not a man whose daughter could barely remember what he looked like. Every call in the weeks leading up to our reunion was like getting a new piece to a complicated puzzle that I would never get the chance to complete. I was not a shy teen and was known for being social, yet when Winston and I spoke, I was reticent to share too much information about who I had grown into as a teen, but I was in a state of wonder about the man who had been folklore in my mind.

Winston and I were strangers bound together only by our shared DNA; my father didn't know me. He didn't know about the stitches I got under my tongue after falling off the bed when I was eight, or that I was considered by teachers as equal parts sweet and scrappy. He didn't know that my greatest fear was a perpetual feeling of not belonging anywhere in this world, a fear surely underscored by his disappearance. I didn't know him either so on the day when he pulled into the driveway of Kyle's house I searched the crevices of my heart trying to bring back the memory of the man whose voice used to soothe me to sleep.

It might have been that my young heart was afraid of being deceived because when my father stepped towards me I asked the question I had stored in the hidden place of my soul — a question that would have wrecked a lesser man, a question I had been too afraid to ask my mother all those years. I moved away from him, placing my hands out in front of me to shield any presence of vulnerability. I turned my face to stare out beyond him and asked, "Where is my father?"

Winston stepped towards the threshold of the door where I perched myself.

"Shakie," he said. "It's me. I'm your father."

I couldn't resist trying to pinpoint what it was about him that led Patsy to fall in love. I wanted to understand what drew her to the man who would break her heart much like the man before him. Maybe it was his posture. Winston's back was straight and steady. He wasn't a very tall man but he carried himself as if he were a giant among men. My father was naturally self-assured and his confidence was contagious. Not long after he came towards me was I standing straight too. If it wasn't his posture that captured my mother's heart, it was most certainly his smile — a smile that we so clearly shared. When he laughed his lips pulled back to the corners of his face just like mine. It would have been difficult to deny me as his progeny: flesh of his flesh and bone of his bone.

Kyle must have noticed my shock because he quickly came and introduced himself as if saving the moment.

"How are you doing sir? I'm Kyle, Shakirah's friend." Kyle said with more bass in his voice than I had ever heard. He extended his hand to shake my father's.

My father's thick Jamaican baritone floated through the living room.

"I jus come fi si mi dahtah," my father said to Kyle, but looking at me.

Our reuniting left us both in a state of transfixion. We stood making small talk like two bypassing neighbors, my mind

Greeted by a Stranger

started to fill with thoughts of getting to know this person with whom I shared so much. The tone of the questions I once coached myself to ask was changing from anger-filled to genuinely curious. I had the opportunity to start over when so many of my peers did not share the same fortune. As these thoughts engulfed my heart, I started experiencing something new; I was beginning to hope.

There was a time when I thought about all the questions I would ask my father if I ever saw him again. Do you love me? Do you think of me? And of course the meta-question: why didn't you try to find me? But, as my father and I spent the three months following our reuniting on Kyle's doorstep getting to know each other those questions became less relevant. Instead, we took long drives with no destinations in mind. We talked about dating and politics and why light travels at the speed it does. He gave me copies of all his favorite books because we shared an insatiable appetite for literature.

One day I came home from school to find his old tennis racket tucked in the corner of my bedroom. It was as if my father was presenting dowry in exchange for my trust. Though I was sometimes reticent about our blossoming relationship, I was grateful for the gifts and even more grateful that he cared enough to try. My mother seemed to enjoy having my father around, too. When he drove down from New York to our home in Maryland, my mom would go out to speak with him. Their conversations often drew her back to the Patsy I never got a chance to know as a child. From my bedroom window, I could see her leaned into my father's car with her body shifted towards him. Her hands supported her head as she laughed an infectious laugh. My father's return brought life back into a dark space.

My tension with Christianity was easing out. I came to embrace Sunday mornings as an opportunity to immerse myself into a piece of Kyle's world. Church offered me a sense of familiarity. I was now one of the congregants clapping to the melody of the gospel songs, mouthing the lyrics as my head moved to the beat. And my body was lighter as if some cosmic force caused me to levitate. Any reservations about God held firm but I permitted myself to be more open-minded. It was, after all, only recently that I had been thinking about my father in church, and then no sooner did he coincidentally make his way back into our lives.

Like every Sunday, Pastor Elliott shared biblical stories. On this particular Sunday, he offered the story of a man named Job in the bible. It is said that God purposefully allowed the devil to take away all of Job's possessions, including his family. As I listened to Pastor Elliott belt out more of his favorite Christian euphemisms I experienced uneasiness with the narrative. The duality of God's vengeance and unconditional love confused me. In an instant, God is described as loving His children and then the next letting the devil kill a man's family. I was trying to find my footing around the idea of faith but it too was complex.

I was beginning to explore the idea that perhaps God had played a role, even if a minor role, in bringing my father to me. Yet, the God who could bring a wayward father home to his teenage daughter was invariably different from the God who was seemingly aloof in the pages of Job. To assuage any lingering anxiety, I pushed my confusion aside to allow in a small fragment of belief. I didn't know what it meant to believe or how belief was going to manifest, particularly in light of the previous hurt I masked. But, if welcoming my father back into my life was a step in the right direction, I wanted to keep going.

My high school graduation came quickly that June. It had been three months since Winston and I reunited. Our relationship was beginning to develop though I remained reluctant to be fully engaged in the kind of father-daughter kinship I desperately desired. It seemed I had good reason to keep my cards close to the chest. When Winston told me he would not be able to attend my graduation, I replied by simply saying it was fine and I would be okay even though it wasn't fine and I wouldn't be okay. The thought of being disappointed by his absence angered me so I did what was natural to me: I buried my feelings.

In the weeks following my graduation, Winston's calls became infrequent. Patsy hardly hid her concern. Each day that passed without hearing from Winston caused her to come into my bedroom asking one question only, "Did you hear from him?" I would shake my head and turn back to the welcome packet I received from the universities I had been accepted to; I had bigger things to focus on. That's what I told myself as a coping mechanism. Should any indication of sadness emerge, I turned it into anger wondering how Patsy could once again be so careless with her children? Why would she allow an inconsistent man back into her daughter's life? Hadn't I been through enough? I hated that I allowed myself to get close to my father. The fact that we shared a bloodline was no longer relevant. He was still a stranger, one who should have remained in the past.

Before long, I returned to autopilot, adding my father's emergence and sudden disappearance to the list of reasons I would learn to protect my own heart. Kyle and I continued dating but our relationship grew fragile as my emotional stability started declining. My temper grew short with his nonchalance and his patience ran up when I could not clearly articulate how devastating it was to be abandoned.

I picked up a summer job as a welcomed distraction and way to save money before leaving for college in August. My father's absence demotivated me from attending church.

The confusion of who God is and what He has the power to do expended me. I didn't want to be like Job or any other character from the bible. I most certainly no longer cared to hear about my proclivity toward sin and how it would be the cause of my eternal destruction if I didn't profess Jesus, Christ as my Lord and savior. There was nothing left for me in the pews of the church. Pastor Elliott would often pray that congregants would leave the church better than they came in. I walked into Kyle's family church with a broken heart and left it all the same.

***

The mall was closed for the evening when the team at Up Against the Wall held another one of our monthly sales meetings. My cell phone was tucked in my backpack, which had been in the breakroom. I didn't know my mother had tried reaching me on it for more than an hour. She rarely called me while I was working so when my store manager handed me the phone in the middle of the meeting I knew something was wrong. I made my way toward the fitting rooms away from my co-workers.

"Hi mommy, is everything okay?" I asked immediately after grabbing the phone from my manager.

"I know you're still at work but I've been trying to reach you. We need to talk —"

"What's going on?" I said, cutting her off.

"Shakirah, it's your father. He died."

My mother's voice cracked as she tried to give me the details of what happened. I couldn't understand what she was saying, all I could feel was a wave of nausea drown me. My body fell back into the bench in the fitting room as if someone had come into the room and pushed me. "I'm coming to get you," I heard Patsy say before I dropped the phone to let out a scream. My manager called out my name asking if everyone was okay. I stumbled out of the fitting room gasping for air as I made my way to the front of the store. My co-workers watched as I charged towards my manager fumbling over my words. "My father—my father is dead."

Patsy pulled into the parking lot of the mall waiting for me. One of my coworkers was kind enough to walk with me to my mother's car. I let the weight of my body sink into her small frame as I walked in agony. Those steps were some of the longest paces I had taken in my young adult life. The moment Patsy saw me coming towards her car, she jumped out and pulled me into her chest. Together we stood in the parking lot wrapped in each other, swaddled in our shared pain. I had lost my father and my mother lost the man she once loved. Why, I asked? Why did this have to happen to us? Patsy didn't respond. Instead, she rubbed my back and helped me into the car.

Winston's return stripped me of my vulnerability. And in the thick of my emotional nakedness, I was robbed of hope. The summer I thought would be spent connecting with friends before we left for our respective schools was replaced by weeks preparing for Winston's wake and funeral in Kingston, Jamaica.

I tried to make sense of his untimely death but could only reckon that our time together wasn't supposed to be cut short. Months before Winston came back into my life, my nights were spent talking to my unborn son. After my father died I replayed over and over our conversations before I went to bed. I thought about the plans I made to visit my father in Queens on the weekends when I could get away from campus. I cried at knowing that he wasn't going to be able to teach me to play tennis with his old tennis racket and that we weren't going to work our way through his favorite book, *The Third Wave*. I regretted that I never got a chance to ask him if he thought of me during his absence from my life and I spent the weeks before his death pouting about his not being at my graduation. I was haunted by his loss.

The wake before my father's funeral was at a small funeral home in Brooklyn. For the first time, I met my uncles, my father's brothers, who all shared his rich, smooth chocolate complexion and almost indiscernible Jamaican Patois. They greeted me with comforting hugs and noted how much I looked like The Dred, as he was called because of his infamous wild hair. Troves of people lined up to see his lifeless body lying in the coffin. I never understood the point of wakes or why anyone would willingly want to see a dead body, especially the body of someone they loved. My mother instructed me to get in line to go see my father before they closed the coffin. It would be the last opportunity I would have to see him, she warned. But I didn't want his fractured face to be my final memory. So, I stood outside watching men and women enter the small room that looked much like the sanctuary of the church I had been attending. Almost all of them came out with tissues pursed to their faces. As they passed me I could hear them whisper that because he had been shot, Winston didn't look like the man who greeted them three months before. He was barely recognizable under the layers of makeup put on him to make him open-casket ready. His once firm and square jaw was crooked from where the first bullet entered.

The funeral worked hard to maintain his facial structure, a challenge made evident by the new cracks in his skin. My father's youngest daughter, Lily, was hiding under her mother's skirt. She had been there when he was killed and was able to get away unharmed. I wondered how she would handle the pain of losing her dad. Would she find a way to erase the vivid images of what happened that day? Or, would she cry in her pillow at night and then go about her

Greeted by a Stranger

life as if it never happened?

As the line dwindled I could see the coffin from outside the funeral home. The sanctuary was adjacent to the parking lot where my uncle and my mother and I sat. My mother was being uncharacteristically attentive, asking me again if I planned to go see my father. She said it as if he was still alive and I was taking a bus trip to visit him. Her helicopter approach made me uncomfortable, not because I couldn't appreciate her efforts to help me grieve but because I didn't want to view my father's body. I wanted to scream in the middle of the parking lot. If I could have clearly articulated the depths of my agony I would have stood on the tallest car and shouted my mourning.

When I looked back in the direction of the funeral home I could see Lily approaching the coffin. Her mother held her hand as she stood on her tippy toes to peak into the coffin. I watched to see if she would cry. She stood for a moment looking as if trying to process why her daddy was laying so still. I knew it would be a matter of time before the tears would begin. Then, I could find satisfaction in knowing she shared in my suffering. The pain wasn't exclusive to me. I waited for the outburst of her emotions to catapult her into a stream of unbridled wailing. The moment never came. Lily's mother picked her up into her arms to whisper into her ear. Without any inclination of being affected in the way one would assume a child who watched her father get murdered would, Lily then waved goodbye to our father, just like she might have waved hello.

I stood looking at my father's disfigured face. The people hadn't lied. He didn't look like the man who came to see me just three months before. His skin looked as if it was made of wax and his body was sunken. I wasn't sure what I was supposed to say. The funeral home cleared and I was the last person standing in the room. The attendant told me to take my time and that when I was ready they would close the coffin for good. I nodded to communicate that I understood. Closing the coffin was going to make his death real, which meant I would have to allow myself the opportunity to mourn him no longer being there and never returning. A closed coffin meant coming to terms with the unresolved issues stemming from my father's return: the unanswered questions and uncertainty of our past as father and daughter. I could have used the moment to tell my father I loved him even though it was hard to comprehend where my love for him came from. And the questions I waited so long to ask could have been presented to his still body. I didn't ask questions or say final words. I walked away from the coffin, leaving it wide open. I wasn't ready to bury the dead.

**

Kyle's mother wasted no time in telling me that she had been praying for me. "Who can understand the ways of God," she said as we sat in her kitchen. I hadn't been sleeping well because I would wake up in the middle of the night thinking my father was standing in my bedroom. The dark rings under my eyes grew more apparent and my hair was shedding abnormally. My temper was growing shorter, too. I tried hard not to roll my eyes at the thought of Mom praying for me. She went on to tell me that even though it hurt, my father's death was a part of God's plan. "It was His will," she said. Those four words caused a burning sensation through my chest. Mom was someone I grew to admire and respect. She welcomed me into her home without hesitation and even though I often despised going to church I admired her faith in what she believed. But on the topic of my father's death, she was breaching closed territory. I thought about barking back to tell her any God who could bring a young woman's father in her life and then snatch

Greeted by a Stranger

him away so shrewdly wasn't a God I wanted to know. As she continued on about the providence and sovereignty of God I daydreamed of letting her know that the Jesus—white skin, blonde hair and blue eyes—Christ she hoped was such a miracle worker, was nothing more than a liar.

I didn't know how to tell Mom that God was nothing more than a wolf in sheep's clothing, wielding no more power than the Great and Powerful Oz. She and her cohort of believers were being peddled a fable. Gods who were good and loving didn't cause people pain. In her diatribe of Christian catchphrases was the suggestion that I come back to church because it would help with my grieving process. Church was the last place I wanted to be. I didn't need to believe in a god to help me cope with my pain. I was managing fine on my own. My life was mine to navigate. If God hadn't made efforts to step into my life before, why would He feel inclined to after the point of impact? Where was this God after my abortion when I cried so much my head felt as if it would explode? Where was he during my mother's verbal assaults? It was too late for me to be assuaged by an unrealistic belief. I had been silly in allowing myself to think a god brought my father back into my life. I didn't have the luxury of writing off my traumas as God's will because they were attached to me. Was simply acknowledging my childhood, abortion and father's death as God's will going to magically take away the hurt? Was it God's will for me to feel empty inside? Did God care that I was alone?

I stopped entertaining the idea of faith. When Kyle asked me about attending church I told him I had to work. It wouldn't be long before I left for school and could be away from the association of my past. My plans for the future fueled me and getting out of Patsy's house — away from the daily reminders of my trauma — was my greatest motivation. I didn't need anyone's help to do that, especially not some God.

Until My Surrender: A Story of Loss, Love and Letting Go

Chapter Four

Is This Love?

Kyle and I spent seven years circling the same block, having the same arguments, and chasing the same false hope that our relationship would get better without either of us changing. I was a mess and I didn't know how badly I was broken until I became Kyle's wife.

Shortly after graduating college, dating Kyle evolved into the shared responsibility of maintaining a marriage and all that comes with its vows. In for better or worse, it seems we were often at worse. I once heard that marriage is like an iceberg. Everything you see in the person you expect to marry is the tip; it's only 10 percent of who they are before the wedding day. After getting married everything you see in the dating stage of the relationship becomes the large portion of the iceberg hidden under water. All of our wonderful and inglorious attributes are exposed in the nakedness of matrimony.

Through my last two years of high school, four years of college, and countless adversity in between, on the day we got married I still couldn't clearly articulate what it was that kept Kyle and me together all those years. Being together was all that we had in common. Over time I had come to see that Kyle was negotiating his own trauma: a dismissive father who died shortly after our wedding and an ill brother whose life also ended too soon. Mom was his only remaining bedrock but not even she could penetrate the layers of deflection with which Kyle armed himself. Kyle buried his secrets so well that I never imagined he could be broken. And it was, perhaps, that my brokenness made Kyle feel a bit less adequate. Our marriage exposed us. Every cracked part of our foundation made vulnerable to the impacts of the iceberg that is matrimony.

When friends who knew us from high school asked the secret to our lasting love I would tell them that being opposites made us attract. We were good for each other in that way, I would say. Those were nothing more than platitudes. After stripping away the superficiality of fleeting emotion—the lip service, the unmerited loyalty and the sex—we were just two dysfunctional people who decided to keep going. Kyle asked me to marry him out of obligation and I said yes out of out an incomplete understanding of what it means to be loved, and not loved just by a man. I didn't know how to be loved by anyone.

On the surface, we appeared to be like any other newlywed couple. The first year is expected to be the hardest. And hadn't Kyle's mother warned us about the perils of living in sin? Without further examination, it would seem that our demise was both statistical and biblical.

I never imagined that I would become someone's wife. The topic of marriage came up while we were both away at our respective universities exchanging emails and instant messages in between classes. Kyle would say that I was wife material, which is to say that I was faithful to him. I was studious—hard working, even. Emotional issues notwithstanding, Kyle could count on me to be there for him. His words were sweet but I never took them seriously until the day he proposed.

We were only a few weeks settled into the condo we purchased together shortly after my graduation from the University of Maryland. September was generous with the weather that year. Summer was well past its expiration date but it lingered and we were all glad for it to do so. I was 17 days shy of my 24th birthday—too young to understand the weight of what would be asked of me by Kyle.

I had been out running errands, looking for trinkets to turn our house into a home. When I arrived back at the condo music was playing.

"Ky, are you home?" I called out into the barely furnished apartment. I could hear movement coming from the back of the condo but Kyle didn't respond. I went to the bedroom to find Kyle standing awkwardly.

"Are you okay?" I asked.

"Come here," Kyle said as he reached his hand out to me.

Kyle was unrecognizable at that moment. There was a softness that I found unsettling. Surprises always made me anxious. I stared at Kyle and walked reluctantly toward him, placing my hand in his.

"Can you sit down?" He asked.

"What is going on, Kyle?" I responded, desperate for some indication of what was happening. He guided me to sit on the bed and kneeled in front on me, resting his arms of my thighs.

"We've been together for a long time now and in that time

we've experienced a lot..."

"I know," I said cutting him off.

"Shakirah, I know it hasn't always been easy but I appreciate you staying by my side all these years."

Kyle continued, "I want you in my life forever."

"You're my best friend. We're always going to be in each other's lives," I responded without thinking about the context or implication of his words.

"I don't want to be your best friend, Shakirah."

Kyle got quiet and took his hand out of mine to reach under the pillow behind me. My face flushed with warmth as my stomach began to bubble like a brook. His hand returned with a small black velvet box. He opened it to showcase a diamond ring.

"I want to be your husband. Will you marry me?" Kyle was the only man I truly knew. Our relationship might not have been built on love but it was familiar and for me, familiar was enough.

"Yes. Yes, I'll marry you."

***

Since moving out of my mother's house we went through a rinse and repeat cycle of speaking and not speaking. On the day I left for good, Patsy and I had an explosive fight that extended from a three-day long disagreement. I was naive to think that it was unlikely my mother would be envious of my relationship with Mom. My yearning for a relationship with Patsy seemed obvious even though she had always seemed so indifferent about connecting with me. She watched me develop a relationship with Kyle's mother, collecting pieces of information like what I purchased Mom for Mother's Day or how often I would spend time with her, to throw back in my face when the opportunity presented itself. When Patsy suggested that I treated Mom better than her I was bewildered. I had only returned the kindness and warmth that Mom gifted me. I was grateful to have a maternal-like-figure to turn to in my growth from a teenager to a young woman.

Patsy's words had always been venomous but one day I broke under the weight of her constant condemnation. She yelled and I yelled back. I stood up for myself in the way I wanted to many times before. I concluded that I would never be good enough for her and we would never have the mother-daughter relationship I desired. I packed my bags and promised never to return. We went a few years without contacting one another throughout my time away at school. She was there for my graduation and I hoped that maybe we could try to rebuild again. When Kyle told me he didn't inform my mother of his intent to marry me, it didn't feel right to leave her in the dark. Even though we remained at odds, I was still my mother's child. She needed to know.

Two weeks went by before I showed up at Patsy's home. My mother was in the kitchen, as usual, fussing over missing dishes that she was certain had been placed in their proper location. "Did they just get up and walk away," she screamed, pointing her question at no one in particular. I stepped into the kitchen and saw that I was now taller than my mother. Her honey brown face was still youthful but age was coming to walk alongside her though she had spent decades evading it.

"What's going on?" Patsy asked with a hint of condescension.

"I have something to tell you," I said.

"Are you pregnant?" She huffed.

"Mommy, I'm not pregnant," I responded, trying to keep

my annoyance at bay.

"I'm getting married," I said.

My mother stopped tending to the pot of curry chicken and turned towards me staring as if waiting for me to deliver a punchline. I held out my hand to show my engagement ring. She pulled my hand close inspecting the ring as if conducting an appraisal.

"When did he propose?" She asked without showing enthusiasm. The steam from the rice and peas mixed with our cutting tension. The kitchen was suddenly becoming sweltering.

"Two weeks ago," I said. Patsy turned back to the stove to sample the chicken. "You know your sister is thinking about going to school."

"That's great," I said before I walking back towards to the door to let myself out.

I couldn't blame Patsy for her lack of excitement. With so few successful marriages in my family, it was no wonder she was reluctant to feign enthusiasm. Then there was the reality that I was becoming everything Patsy likely believed I could be and in doing so, my realization as a woman coming into my own was reminding her of her own shortcomings. Each of Patsy's three marriages ended in divorce. Almost all of the women in my family were single mothers yet there I was standing in her kitchen flashing an engagement ring — her child who went off to college, who moved out at 18 and who was decidedly too ambitious to remain under the curse of the women in the Hill family. It was Patsy who had planted the seed that I could obtain more for myself. The day she asked me to decide between leaving her home or aborting my baby, I believed we entered into an unspoken agreement. In exchange for my child, I would chart on a new trajectory that our family hadn't yet seen. When Patsy brushed off my engagement to Kyle, I suspected she might have expected me to trip up somewhere along the way. I felt strongly that even though my mother believed me to be her special child, she held out hope that I would keep myself boxed in to be just like her.

***

Kyle recommended we attend premarital counseling before getting married. I didn't see the purpose in talking to a stranger about the intricacies of our marriage before we were even married. I could think of a million more pressing things for Kyle and me to focus on leading up to the big day. Even though seeking outside help made me feel weak, I knew it was important to Kyle. Kyle's Godfather agreeing to counsel us gave me some ease. Our first session involved Pastor Elliott asking us a series of questions about our relationship: how long we had been dating, how we fell in love. That sort of thing. It was fun to recount the story of Kyle reluctantly fixing my computer in Mrs. P's class. But the session took an interesting turn when Pastor Elliott brought God into the conversation. I shouldn't have been surprised by the turn in direction. Pastor Elliott was a man of the cloth after all.

"Why do you want to get married?" he asked.

Kyle and I sat silently because the answer seemed obvious. I looked at Kyle to see if he would be the one to state what was clear. When he didn't respond I offered my declaration.

"We love each other," I said as a matter of fact.

"Of course you do," Pastor Elliot said smiling and reclining in his brown leather chair.

As his question hung in the air unanswered like a riddle on a game show I started to look around his tiny church office. It was old and dusty filled with books that haven't been read in more than a decade. There was a large bible resting on the corner of Pastor Elliott's desk. I wondered if he referenced it when speaking one-on-one with the members of his flock or if it were there for show.

"I mean, why else would we get married?" Kyle boldly asked.

There were few times Kyle and I agreed on this. Much of our dialogue consisted of opposing arguments. If I said left, Kyle would say right without fail. But my motion backed his question. Why else would two people get married? Isn't that what all the best romance movies and books purported— love so great two people feel no other choice than to spend their lives together?

"Love..." Pastor Elliott's voice sang in staccato as he continued"...is a great catalyst for two people coming together, but it cannot sustain a marriage."

Suddenly the room grew thick with tension. Kyle and I were being confronted with a truth neither of us were prepared to hear.

"Marriage was not created for the sole purposes of love. It was made to glorify God. Do you understand that?"

I didn't understand, but I nodded my head as if I did. I was tired of God always making an unwanted appearance in my life. I had given Him my Sundays. Now once again He was asking me to use my marriage to glorify Him. What did that even mean anyway? Pastor Elliott challenged Kyle and me to think about how our pending marriage could glorify God, but all I could think about was how to avoid coming back to pre-marital counseling.

***

We were a few weeks out from our wedding when the evening of Kyle's bachelor party came around. I spent the night alone in the condo plagued with anxiety. Thoughts zipped through my mind as I considered all the arguments we left unresolved. Kyle never bought me flowers and asking him to do chores was more exhausting than doing the chore itself. I had long suspected the lack of bonding between Kyle and me wasn't normal for a couple who was planning to wed. And Pastor Elliott's ridiculous notion that somehow, in the midst of our ridiculous relationship, we were expected to glorify God. God who conveniently only showed up when He felt like it.

I sent Kyle a text asking when he planned to come home. Two hours would pass before I received a response, a terse reply that was better left unsent. Kyle was stonewalling again. He was shutting me out at the moment when I needed him to let me in. The reassurance I hoped would come through digitized words of affirmation didn't flash across the screen of my iPhone. I wanted to know if I was making the right decision, because ever since Pastor Elliott's counseling the nagging sensation living in the pit of my stomach through the duration of our relationship, grew stronger.

"What if he never changes?" I called Starria as a last resort.

It was either belt out my frustrations to the first of my girlfriends who answered their phone or crash Kyle's bachelor party. I was panicking but didn't know why.

"You have cold feet. That's natural, Shakirah. Everyone experiences that before they get married."

Starria was one of my college friends. Sitting in sophomore English at the University of Maryland we shared jokes on having West Indian parents. Starri and I equally knew all the appropriate Jamaican colloquialisms and their context. But our upbringings were completely different. Her parents had been married for more than two decades, something I had never thought was possible. So when I needed advice on my relationship I trusted Starria. If for no other reason than her having seen what a real marriage is supposed to look like. Usually, Starria's advice was spot on. She's talked me off many ledges when I was ready to abandon my relationship with Kyle. This time my impulses were screaming louder than Starria's wisdom.

Having cold feet was an easy answer, but what I was battling had deeper roots. Kyle came home to find me curled up in our walk-in closet. When I suffered major anxiety attacks I hid in enclosed spaces as a way of shutting out the pain. Ironically, I was locking myself in with the trauma. He knelt at my side in the same way he did on the day he proposed. The softness around his eyes came back again.

"You're scared aren't you?" He asked while pulling my head to his chest.

"Yes," I said. Scared wasn't giving full context to the reticence I was experiencing.

Hours before Kyle came home I was pulling up spreadsheets to call our wedding guests one by one to let them know the wedding was off. And like always, Kyle wasn't privy to this plan. It didn't matter. He would've gone along with calling off the wedding, showing just as much passion as a snail. Kyle didn't get worked up about me, or our wedding, or our future. And that was a part of the problem. No matter how much I pined I couldn't tell whether or not he truly loved me.

"I'm scared too," Kyle said as he wiped the tears from my eyes. If pending matrimony was making me an even more neurotic nut case, it was making Kyle a vulnerable man.

"What if we end up hating each other?" I asked.

"Then we'll just hate each other for life. No divorce." Kyle said half smiling.

"No divorce?" I asked. "Are you sure you want to spend forever with me?"

"I know that people make marriage sound like a death sentence, but I want to do it with you."

Other couples had fiery passion, romance and perhaps even God. Kyle and I had each other. Maybe that was enough. In the shower the next morning I said a prayer. "God, I'm sure I'm the last person you want to hear from and I know we haven't been on the best terms, but I need a favor. If Kyle isn't the man for me can you please show me?"

***

I couldn't see when all the pieces were adding up until it was too late. From our engagement to an inability to answer Pastor's Elliot's question about why we were planning to marry each other.

It's often said the first year of marriage is the hardest. I wouldn't describe our first year as being hard, but it was definitely empty. Our living room that was once the battlefield for the civil war in our relationship was now the passing grounds. Kyle and I weren't arguing, which would've been a good thing if it meant our problems subsided. We weren't arguing but we also weren't growing any closer. I gave up trying to convince Kyle to be a more emotionally involved partner. I bought my own flowers and went for long walks alone. If I had been more present in my marriage I would've seen that Kyle was struggling. In the span of three years his brother and father died. The losses pushed a naturally reserved Kyle into a darker space. I wanted to help him grieve, but after eight years I still hadn't come to terms with my father's death. We hadn't learned to support one another through tragedy. Being in his presence wasn't enough.

Kyle grew temperamental, going from not emoting to exploding over the most trivial of things. When I wanted to paint an accent wall in our living room Kyle told me I was being irrational and irresponsible. To me, it was just a wall, but to Kyle, there was too much change. I created peace between us by surprising Kyle with a 48-inch flat screen television in time for football season.

I was suffocating in our marriage and growing frustrated with myself for being too needy. The emotional bags I had been carrying were growing too heavy, but when I looked around there was nowhere for me to unpack them. All the memories of my past welded like fire shut up in my bones. I never envisioned marriage but I made attempts at what I thought was a good wife. I cooked most evenings and kept our house clean, almost to Kyle's disdain. I encouraged Kyle to date me. But, I could sense Kyle was frustrated with me too. The time I requested we spend together was replaced by the television. Dinner parties and family events were spent alone. I got very clever at making excuses for Kyle's absence. I didn't know how to stop the runaway train, so I kept maintaining and pretending like what little I had of Kyle's heart hadn't slipped away.

Kyle's best friend Jackson suggested we spend New Year's Eve with him and his new fiancé, Noori. Jackson had been telling us about Noori for the last few months and how they were doing their relationship "God's way." I met Noori once before at a charity event the guys hosted each year as part of their budding nonprofit. It was clear why Jackson had asked her to be his wife. Noori was objectively beautiful: big brown eyes, long jet-black hair. Though she had the physical presence of a model, her countenance was less intimidating. Noori spoke sweetly of Jackson in a way that I had never seen his previous girlfriends do. I liked Noori for Jackson. I hadn't known her for long but the feeling in my gut moved towards peace when I saw them together.

I was nervous that Kyle would decline Jackson's invite and I didn't want to spend another boring evening in the house. "It's New Year's Eve," I said to Kyle. "We should go to dinner with them. Let's have some fun."

For once convincing Kyle was easy because no sooner than I worked up my dissertation on why we needed to not be the young married couple stuck in the house on a holiday, Kyle called Jackson to get the details on dinner.

Noori and Jackson regaled us with how sweet their first encounter was as the clock moved us closer to 2011. The restaurant was packed with couples all wanting to bring in the new year with overpriced champagne and hors d'oeuvres. Jackson talked about the roles of God and prayer in their decision to get married. Jackson and Kyle were both raised in Christian households, but I had never heard a man speak about his faith with as much conviction as Jackson. Likewise, Noori rested her hand on Jackson's lap nodding in agreement with his stance. Her gentle voice chimed in as she shared that the couple was waiting for their wedding day to have their first kiss. "For us, this is the best way to honor God." Noori said. Few things shocked me, but hearing their story left me speechless. I had questions, yet they periled in the face of Jackson and Noori's resolve. Kyle was equally shocked but he decided to take the low road asking questions filled with more cynicism than curiosity.

"So, you feel like you have something to prove to God, Jackson? Waiting until your wedding day to kiss just seems like overachieving."

"Nah, man," Jackson said. "Noori is a gift. You treat good gifts with care. And besides, for all the ways God has demonstrated His love for us, this is the least we can do."

Following dinner, Jackson and Noori invited Kyle and me to a New Year's Eve party hosted by the couple's ministry at their church. We arrived at what looked like a mansion in

Fort Washington where, on the inside, the atmosphere was warm. Husbands gathered together in the living room to talk about work and sports. The women congregated around the dining room table where the conversation centered on rearing children. At the table sat Mrs. Grace, the wife of Jackson and Noori's pastor. She was a petite woman with a quiet presence. When she did speak her words were selective. These people, Christian men, and women, were different from what I saw represented in the few churches I attended. There were young couples like Kyle, Jackson, Noori and me and there were older couples. They didn't use long Christian dialogue in their conversation. They were normal people who had, in the community of their faith, found what I was searching for all along—love.

I wondered the secret to their peace as we gathered in the living room for prayer as the clock struck midnight. A tall, dark man entered the room.

"I feel it appropriate as we go into another year to start 2011 off with prayer." Judging by his presence and everyone's immediate notice of him, he was Jackson and Noori's pastor.

"I'm gonna let the Holy Spirit lead me as I pray, so if everyone could bow your heads and close your eyes, let's make room for God to speak." A circle was formed as couples locked hands. I looked over at Kyle to see if he would make the first move towards the front door, but his head was bowed and his hand was reaching out for mine.

I reluctantly bowed my head hoping this would be over quickly. The pastor walked in the middle of the circle speaking to couples. His words weren't formed into normal prayer. He was telling the couples things about their future. I looked up to find the pastor standing parallel to Kyle and me. The couple he was speaking to nodded in agreement at his words. As he finished speaking with the couple across from Kyle and me a voice in my head that sounded like my own whispered, *he's coming to you next*. I put my head down to find the pastor's feet headed in our direction.

"Is this your wife?" Pastor Rubio asked Kyle.

"Yeah," I heard Kyle say. I kept my head down not wanting to entertain whatever was about to take place.

Pastor Rubio began speaking things about our lives that no one could have known. I wondered what we had gotten ourselves into by agreeing to come to this party. Did Jackson and Noori set us up?

"You're lukewarm right now and God wants to make you hot," Pastor Rubio said before beginning to pray over us.

Once again I was confronted with God except for this time it came with a direct request. God wanted to make us hot. I was clueless as to what that meant, but I was growing tired of this cat and mouse game we were playing. On the car ride home, Kyle and I remained silent. Jackson and Noori were ecstatic over our prophecy.

"What's a prophecy?" I asked from the backseat.

"It's when God speaks something to you through a person."

I glanced at Kyle to see if he would offer any perspective. He was looking out the window, staring into the early morning sky. What was in that head? Better yet, what was in that heart?

January brought in a harsh winter—colder than the years prior. Kyle and I lay in bed wrapped in our favorite down comforter. We hadn't talked about what Pastor Rubio said about our relationship and God wanting to make us hot. Kyle's King James Bible rested on his nightstand next to a picture of us on our wedding day. Since the start of the New Year, we had been in a good place. It was as if a tide was turning in our marriage. Kyle rolled over moaning in what sounded like pain.

"Ky, what are you doing?" I asked as I pulled at his arms to draw his body into mine. He turned over with tears in his eyes.

"I'm so unhappy," he said.

"What?" I pulled Kyle up to face me.

"What are you talking about? What's wrong?"

"Shakirah, I'm not happy. I haven't been happy for a long time."

I couldn't believe what was coming out of Kyle's mouth. After all the fighting and frustration we were finally starting to get closer. I thought the New Year had brought us new promise, but Kyle was sobbing uncontrollably. As we sat together in our bedroom where Kyle had proposed two years before I tried to repair the breach. I tried to stop Kyle's tears but they kept coming like a broken dam.

"Is this about Rick and your father?" I asked trying to make sense of Kyle's sudden breakdown.

"No, Shakirah. It's you." Kyle words shout out his mouth like a dart aimed at the bullseye. They were sharp and without explanation. I let the sting of the moment hit me while Kyle continued crying.

"I don't love you anymore," he said. "I don't love you."

***

Part II: This is My Surrender

Chapter Five

Cut To the Bone

Kyle's sudden absence intensified the sting of winter. Waking each morning since he announced his displeasure with our marriage felt like trying to escape a never-ending nightmare. I would stretch my arms toward his pillow only to find that his side of the bed was cold.

The days without Kyle home were long. And for many of those days — weeks even— I replayed the events leading up to his departure trying to find a hint, some inclination that this turn of events was inevitable. I had been correct to look for evidence of where we might have gone awry but I was misguided to assume that it was an isolated incident that led us to estrangement. I was blinded by my own subconscious refusal to see that though Kyle was a physical presence, he never truly invested deeply in our relationship. Kyle was gone before I made our relationship official the summer he left for college. He was gone before we purchased our condo. He was gone before dropping down on one knee asking me to be his wife and he was gone before we said I do. When Kyle sent me an instant message to tell me that he would not be coming home — all he was taking from me by then was his body, his heart had already been long gone.

Blaming the toxicity of our relationship on youthfulness would have been easy. It's true that in high school we were too immature to manage the undertaking of a relationship. Youth plays a role in the breakdown of our household but only a marginal one. Had Kyle and I been another couple — a couple with an equal investment not only in the marriage but also in the work that we both required to heal our pasts — we could have overcome the subterfuge that lay ahead. But, for the first time, I was seeing that I had always been alone. I was carrying the last name of a man who convinced himself marrying was the right thing to do. Our marriage, I learned, was never meant to be and so trying to fix it was elusive. I tried anyway.

***

Kyle and I were well acquainted with the vicious cycle of emotional and psychological abuse. It hadn't occurred to me that our patterns of withdrawal, retaliation and at times physical abuse were abnormal. Couples fight, I assumed. Yet, our battles never brought us to win the war. We were no more enlightened as a result. Offenses were silenced by sex and exhaustion. Never did we soul search.

We sat together in church each Sunday and remained ignorant to the lessons that we could have easily applied to ourselves and in turn our marriage. We never examined our shortcomings the way a doctor who is desperately trying to diagnose an ill patient would. I settled for the sprints of silence that would befall our tiny home, and in those moments, I convinced myself that we were good. Kyle's exit snapped me into recognizing that things were bad; things were really bad. I couldn't see it then but Kyle's leaving was one of the greatest gifts God would grant me; it was then that I was forced to see how deep my scars were. In his absence, I came into the reckoning of all the trauma I endured. Like a shipwreck survivor, I was removed from the infliction of my pain but it was in the stillness of night when I cried out for answers that God showed me I was cut to the bone.

I was too embarrassed to tell my friends that Kyle and I were separated out of fear of being judged. They would find out eventually but in the immediate weeks I was alone I only reached out to Noori, Jackson's fiancé. When I shared with Noori that Kyle and I were separated she gave me such compassion that it was like drinking cold water after enduring a bout of dehydration. Noori, whose name means "the light," was consistently patient with me on the days I would call or text her with my despair.

"This is really hard Noori. And I'm more than hurt." I said during one of our conversations.

"I can only imagine. I do know that your husband loves you, Shakirah. You have to hold onto the belief that he loves you and that God is not surprised by this. God is for you and for Kyle."

I was desperate to believe what Noori said about Kyle was true. I held out for a sign that he did love me and somehow our love would bring us back together. Noori talked a lot about God being a restorer and that when the time was right God would make our marriage better than it had been before. Noori taught me to hope for the salvation of my marriage and the deliverance of my soul. Only one of the two would come to pass.

The evolution of my friendship with Noori surprised us both but immediately proved to beneficial. With Kyle no longer spending his nights at home, Noori was able to stay with me while she and Jackson prepared for their wedding.

Cut To the Bone

They were diligent in not sleeping together. I was grateful that I could offer my home as a small token of gratitude for the way Noori showed up for me. As I heard more about Noori's life and how she came into her faith, I discovered more of what it was to have a relationship with God.

"A relationship with God is different than calling yourself a Christian," Noori explained during one of our sleepovers. She stretched her long legs across the living room floor with a bible across her lap. Her voice was delicate and deliberate.

"But Noori, how can you have a relationship with someone you can't see?" I asked sheepishly.

"It's strange right…?" Noori let out a jovial laugh as though she was looking back to the time when she asked similar questions.

"The relationship is different than the ones we have here on earth. We fellowship with God through our worship and our obedience. Then He comes into our hearts. He changes us and because we love God we are happy to let Him change us."Noori said all this while posturing her hands over heart.

"What about the rules?" I asked.

"When you have a relationship with God you stop seeing obedience as a rule following and recognize that what He calls us to is for our benefit more so than His."

I hung to Noori's words like they were the only meal that could satisfy me. God had never been explained in this way before. The more questions Noori answered, the more I became curious about starting a relationship with God.

Noori had previously invited me to join her for what she called a small group. "It's a chance for women to come together and learn more about their relationship with God," Noori said on the day she made her initial pitch. I was reluctant then but because Kyle and I regularly attended Mom's newly founded church as a couple, going there as a place of respite felt futile. Despite my reservations, I dropped my guard and decided I would take Noori up on her offer.

The evening was crisp when I walked the mile from my condo towards the student apartments. The neighborhood where we purchased our home was changing. I was so engrossed in the fallout of my marriage that I didn't notice the new rowhomes being developed. Though my life felt it was regressing, the world continued forward. I entered the recreation room of the University Towers and grabbed a seat in one of the chairs that had been arranged in a circle. A woman with deep dark skin and high cheekbones greeted me.

"Hi, are you here for Sister Circle?" she asked.

"Small group?" I said.

"Yes, our small group is called Sister Circle. The church is still working on finding the right name for our groups. I'm Van," she said while extending her hand.

"I'm Shakirah," I said, taking Van's hand into mine.

"Ohhh —Shakirah. You're Kyle's wife, right? I'm Brenden's fiance."

"I thought you looked familiar," I said as other women began entering.

"How did you hear about Sister Circle?" she asked while smiling at the women who began sitting one by one.

"Noori, " I said.

Ten women sat in a circle sharing their stories of struggling with doubt. I listened as they poured out their frustrations to one another like milk into coffee. I liked that they were honest with themselves about their shortcomings. Their forthrightness was not helpless like the times my mother was berating my siblings and me. The women were not

Cut To the Bone

bitter though they often admitted how difficult it was to keep bitterness at bay. This degree of vulnerability was palatable. They were not victims. They were simply women trying to edge closer to divinity. In the many instances God came into the conversation, He was not depicted as a power-wielding dictator. To the women in Sister Circle, God was their friend, father, and closest companion. God was a noble gentleman who pursued their hearts and waited patiently for their acquiescence. We spent the evening reading pieces of the Bible that related to each women's doubts. I had imagined that I would feel out of place among women who were staunchly rooted in their Christian convictions. It pleased me to see that I was wrong. I felt at ease in Sister Circle. As the night came to a close, we took turns praying for each other. A young woman to my left turned to me with a wide-eyed smile, the same kind of smile my father and I shared on the day we reunited and asked how should she pray for me.

I whispered, "Please pray for my husband." I said before I bowed my head in anticipation of better things to come.

***

Kyle and I had been separated for a month by the time my life came into a new routine. During the workday, I exchanged emails with him demanding answers to how we could get past our separation. Kyle's responses were always dismissive. I don't love you and I don't think I ever loved you, he would reply. Some days I was able to self-govern with ease. It took equal parts restraint and avoidance to make it through 24 hours without having an emotional breakdown. Then there were days I went ballistic, calling Kyle's phone crying hysterically. I begged him to come home. This was also a confusing time. Kyle's belongings remained intact, hanging neatly in the closets. His work shoes lined the doorway. When I asked Kyle to get his belongings he told me no without any explanation as to why. I thought this was his way of saying he would return.

As the sun exchanged shifts with the moon I oscillated from abandoned wife to an eager pupil wanting to learn more about the truth of God and His son Jesus. I started reading the bible and rehearsing scriptures that brought comfort to my aching. The Psalms were poetic and the Proverbs enriching. I flipped through the Gospels to see that Jesus' words were inked in red. *We love [God] because He first loved us,* I inscribed in my bible. I searched the holy book for answers on how to approach my failing marriage. I wanted to know if I should let go or if I should hold on. I needed assurance that if I fought for my marriage Kyle would come back to me and that we could be better than before as Noori said. Prayer also became central to my new routine. Noori told me that praying was nothing more than having a conversation with God. During those nights when the pain was most intense, God and I had a lot of conversations.

As the weeks passed, holding onto my newfound hope of a restored marriage and a loving husband was growing tiresome. I walked into the bedroom where I had left a laundry basket filled with our clean clothes resting by our bedside. I was annoyed at myself for forgetting to put the clothes away. You're a mess. It's no wonder Kyle left you, I thought to myself. And then the echoing of Kyle's hurtful words pushed me to my knees. *I don't love you. I never loved you.* The words pierced deeper into my heart. Kyle's words tangled with the words my mother who would often say: *You make me sick. I wish I never had you.* Soon, I couldn't differentiate their voices. Kyle's words reminded me of my mother and my mother's words reminded me of Kyle.

I was breathless, panting for acknowledgment of my hurt. "What do you want...?" I yelled into the silence of the condo.

Cut To the Bone

"What do you want—?" My voice was growing louder. My body burned as sadness turned into inconsolable anger. I pounced the laundry, grabbing as many as pieces of garments my hands could contain. Tossing them in the air with rage, my crying morphed to screaming. I threw the empty basket aside creating space, making room for someone to engage me in this battle of one. I looked toward the ceiling. My tears wet the back of my neck and dropped on my shoulders like rain hitting the roof on a stormy night. My chest heaved as I screamed again. "What do you want from me?" My voice echoed back from the hollowness of our home. There was no response. The wind whipped past the bedroom window, haunting the moment with all my fears and sadness still yet to come.

***

Noori sat in the dining room with concentrated poise.

"When's the last time you spoke to Kyle?" she asked.

"Wednesday," I said. We've been talking about marriage counseling. He seems reluctant, so I don't know."

Fatigue highlighted the dark circles around my eyes. Pants that normally hugged my hips were barely keeping around my waist. If Noori was concerned about the change in my appearance she hid it well.

"Have you given any thought to what Pastor Rubio said?" It didn't seem like an appropriate moment to talk about what happened at the New Year's Eve party, but I entertained the question because I had been giving a lot of thought to the prophecy spoken over Kyle and me.

"I just don't know what it means, Noori. All of this is too much. I can't take it anymore." Noori leaned in and placed her hand over mine.

"I know. I'm really sorry you're dealing with this right now. Would you feel okay coming to church with me?" She asked. Since attending small group had gone so well I trusted that church would be an extension of the relief I experienced.

"Sure," I said.

The Saturday before I visited Holy Gates Church, Noori gave me the rundown of what to expect. She told me that the church was in a movie theater, a detail so peculiar I was certain I misheard. Pastor Rubio who Kyle and I met on New Year's Eve was the church's lead pastor. She noted that Brenden and Van would be familiar faces in the crowd and if I wanted I could sit with them. Since Brenden and Jackson were Kyle's longtime friends, I decided it was best not to tell him I would be attending their church. I was afraid he would see my attendance as a form of manipulation; that perhaps I was using this as a way to bring him back home. I concluded he needed fewer reasons to resent me. My visitation would remain between Noori, Jackson, Van, Brenden and me.

I arrived for service at Holy Gates and confirmed that the church was, in fact, in a movie theater. The greeters at the theater check-in were warm. "Welcome to Holy Gates," one greeter said while pointing me toward the sanctuary. Young men and women who appeared my age stood around talking before the service began. Everyone looked close and familiar. It had been a long time since I was around a large group of people. I made my way to theater nine, which transformed into a sanctuary every Sunday when I spotted Pastor Rubio in the distance. I wondered if he would recognize me as the young woman he had given the prophecy to two months prior. The ushers at the entrance of theatre nine directed me to my seat. A young band played Christian rock music as men and women stood to their feet with their hands stretched in the air. They looked as if they transcended into another place and time. The theater

Cut To the Bone

screen displayed the lyrics to the songs being sung by the worship team. Immediately following singing, a gentleman made brief announcements as Pastor Rubio made his way down to theater's front, center.

Arriving on time for service meant that I would be sitting in the front row. When Pastor Rubio glanced in my direction before delivering his sermon, I locked my eyes on him to see if he would recall me. He gave no inclination of remembrance. Pastor Rubio was a tall and regal man who walked with trustful command. His stride wasn't arrogant but it was self-assured. He pushed his suit jacket back, placed his hands in his pockets as he faced the congregation.

"Good morning, Church." He roared.

"Good morning," the congregation repeated.

"Today, I want to bring your attention a man named David. He was known as being a man after God's own heart." Pastor Rubio pulled out his phone and scrolled.

Pastor Rubio had no trouble keeping his congregation's attention. It wasn't that he was a pastor. His brand of spiritual celebrity was that he was a man who God found broken. Pastor Rubio's brokenness, his own story of betrayal and restoration was the thesis of his pastoral platform. Few pastors were as transparent and humble as he was with his congregation. Pastor Rubio evaded the pomp and circumstance that allured young pastors of his stature. He knew how to read his room and was careful to follow the direction of what Christians call the Holy Spirit. And he was well aware that because much of his church attendance came from college students and the city's young professionals, he had to remain relatable. His words were a mix of dignity, doxology, and D.C. twang.

"Please open your bibles—whether that's on your cell phones, or mobile device is fine by me—" The crowd laughed at the accuracy of knowledge Pastor Rubio's had about his congregation. Within minutes iPads, iPhones, and other electronic devices lighted the room. "Turn to Psalm 40," Pastor Rubio continued. "I think what God loved so much about David was not that he was a king. I think what God loved about David is that even as a king he humbled himself before God. I wonder where else in the bible we see this kind of submission."

"Jesus!" Someone yelled.

"Jesus." Pastor Rubio parroted before continuing his sermon.

"See, we can get caught up in our lives and miss the very thing God has for us—Himself."

I followed along as we Pastor Rubio read through the Psalm. What I once saw as dense words from an antiquated book came alive during his sermon.

"In Psalm 40 David learns what it means to give God what's most important to Him, ourselves. Church, there is an exchange we have to participate in when we come before God, but it's not the kind of exchange we think. Let's keep reading..."

...Sacrifice and offering you did not desire, but my ears you have pierced; burnt offerings and sin offerings you did not require. Then I said, 'Here I am...'

-Psalm 40

The words of the scripture slid through a crack in my heart like an uninvited, yet much welcomed guest. As Pastor Rubio proceeded with his sermon, I recalled the night I had cried out to God asking what He wanted from me. I had expected the voice of God would descend from the sky and meet in the laundry basket like Moses and the burning bush or that He would come from behind a screen like the Great and Powerful Oz. God did not show up that night but in a small theater filled with hundreds of young people who wanted more of Him, He was responding. Through Pastor Rubio's words that Sunday morning, God was being a noble gentleman, making his proposition known. "Sometimes—" Pastor Rubio's voice ascended, the room moved their eyes between him and illuminated screens. We hung in anticipation, baited by the eloquence of King David's words. Pastor Rubio dug deeper into his sermon: "Sometimes, we think we can offer God our stuff as if our 'stuff' can take place of being in a relationship with Him. God doesn't want your stuff. He wants your heart. If God has your heart, He can transform your life. He won't allow this transformation to happen a moment sooner."

As the sermon came to a close Pastor Rubio paced the theater. "There are those of you who haven't given God what's so precious to Him. You've been trying to replace Him with stuff or with people. You've been holding on to your baggage and God is telling you to come. If that's you, I want to pray for you today." I bowed my head and closed my eyes. Trying to stop emotion from overtaking me was pointless so I let my tears flow as they had done every night since my separation began. The days and weeks had been difficult to weather. I was beyond exhausted. There was nowhere else to turn. I was without the support of my family. Kyle's vitriol was increasing. I didn't know what would happen after that moment. Maybe nothing would change. Maybe everything would get worse. I didn't care. Pastor Rubio's prayer drifted into the background while I imagined myself extending my hand to accept the Noble Gentlemen's invitation.

"Here I am. Here I am."

Chapter Six

Dark Night of the Soul

C hristians don't tell you that when you enter a relationship with God that you'll pendulum swing from feeling incredibly high to the disturbingly low. This phenomenon might be the result of so many of us coming into this relationship when we've hit rock bottom or as theologians call it, the Dark Night of the Soul.

My new adoption of Christianity was beautiful to those who were familiar with the process of transformation. For those who didn't fully understand what it meant to "give your heart to God," transformation looked crazy. I was abandoning old habits. On the weekends I tossed any semblance of what I started referring to as *my life before Christ*. Articles of clothing that appeared too revealing were stuffed into garbage bags. Old CDs by artists whose music would make the saints blush were tossed into the trash can.

The only artist I could not depart from was Beyoncé. Beyoncé grew up in the church. She was Christian, I bargained. Her music remained.

I was exorcizing my demons while God was making me new. Christian vocabulary became my new language. When I was spending time with new friends from Holy Gates we were fellowshipping. Waking up in the morning to read the bible and pray was my devotion time. Going without food and water for predetermined periods of time meant that I was fasting to hear from God. Fasting was a tool to which I relied on heavily. Kyle and I were still at an impasse. When I could not get answers from him or our marriage counselor, I fasted to seek answers from God.

The journaling habit I adopted as a teen served me well during my transformation. The notebook that was once filled with poetry and the ruminations of a heartbroken young woman were replaced by the written prayers of a long-suffering wife. I wrote letters to Jesus asking Him to soften Kyle's heart towards me. For a moment it appeared that my prayers were being answered because on a random Saturday afternoon, Kyle came home.

I returned from lunch with an old friend to find Kyle seated at the edge of our bed. "What are you doing here?" I asked.

"I'm home," Kyle said looking disappointed.

"Okay, but why?"I asked.

"I just wanted to come home." He said sharply before making his way to the bathroom. I heard the hissing of water coming from the faucets as I stood at the center of the bedroom in disbelief.

Kyle's actions were consistently confusing during our time apart. He told me that he was no longer in love with me and that I made him unhappy in our marriage but sent an orchid on Valentine's Day. When I called to ask if his gesture meant he wanted to work on repairing our marriage Kyle told me that I was reading too much into the gift. He had only sent the plant because he knew no one else would give me anything on Valentine's Day. It was a pity purchase. I was crushed by his words but tended to the orchid with delicacy. I placed it on Kyle's side of the bed as a totem. He was being stubborn. He would be home, I convinced myself.

Kyle's return did not bring promise that our marriage was on an upward trajectory. During the few days he stayed home he was distant and mean when I reached out to him for connection. I was accustomed to Kyle's sarcasm but he was even more biting so much so that I couldn't escape the idea that he was trying to hurt me.

"I invited some people over to watch the game tomorrow." I was stunned that Kyle could act as if we were not in a moment of crisis. I wanted to object but I was afraid I might push him further away. I silently agreed with God that I would remain peaceful and win Kyle over with my new, transformed heart. I hoped he would see that I was working to become a better woman, a reformed wife that was capable of making him happy. Kyle was not impressed. The scriptures I left on Post It notes throughout the condo were a punchline.

"Don't be like those people in prison," Kyle said while we made our way through the grocery store to shop for snacks.

"What are you talking about, Kyle?"

"People in prison — they mess up and then to turn to God hoping He will get them out of prison." I wasn't following Kyle's logic.

"I'm not sure what this has to do with me."

"You're saying you're Christian now but if we don't work out — I just don't want this to be the reason you're turning

Dark Night of the Soul

to God."

I couldn't deny that I hoped an extension of God's mercy meant He would restore my marriage. My prayers for Kyle were sincere. Even more than sincere prayers for Kyle was my devotion to God. I hoped Kyle and I could work things out and I was pressing God for answers. But I wasn't looking for a genie when I walked into Holy Gates. I was looking for direction. As juvenile as I was in my faith, I had learned quickly that God is kind enough to grant guidance to people who ask for direction.

I slid back into my domesticity easily, making plates and attending to our guests who crammed into the living room. I even made Kyle's plate and walked it to him as he watched the game. Where I staggered was trying to sit by Kyle's side and pretend like things were back to normal. It felt dishonest to have our friends over without as much as discussing what it meant for Kyle to be home. He offered that he was back because he wanted to be home but it was unclear whether he wanted to be home with *me*.

Throughout the night I caught glimpses of Noori and Jackson who were snuggled up on the bench basking in the glow of their forthcoming nuptials. I longed for the kind of bond they shared and wondered if Kyle and I could have that kind of closeness. That kind of love seemed out of reach for Kyle and me but I was glad for Noori. She was happy and had become invested in her happiness. Every so often Noori and I would exchange glances. She would shoot me a playful wink as if to say, *You got your man back. Things are good. Can't you see?* What Noori didn't know is that when everyone left the apartment he switched back into a stranger I barely recognized.

That night we laid in bed, I was nervous to be physically vulnerable again but when Kyle reached out for me I gave my body over to him. I believed that making love after all the months of fighting could soften the intensity. Sadly, our intimacy was different than it had been all the times we made love before. I could sense that Kyle was checked out. My suspicions were confirmed when I tried initiating a conversation as we sprawled across the duvet with the sheets sketching over our frames.

"Kyle, can we please talk about what's going on?" I made sure to keep my voice soft as an acknowledgment of our physical and emotional nakedness.

"I don't really want to talk about this, Shakirah." He quipped.

"To be honest. I'm confused. You're back here and we're having sex —"

"You're an attractive woman. Of course, I'm going to want to have sex with you." Kyle said before turning his back to me.

Kyle's emotional blows were becoming frequent and more intense. I didn't respond. Instead, I made my way to the living room and crawled onto the couch to cry myself to sleep. Kyle came behind me.

"You don't have to sleep on the couch, Shakirah."

"What do you expect me to do?" I asked.

"Can we not do this tonight," Kyle said.

"Are you f—ing serious?" I screamed, jumping up from the couch. "You walked your ass out of here without any explanation. All you keep saying is that you don't love me. You're sending me flowers. If I don't call you then you call me. But if I ask for answers you push me away. What is this sh—t?"

"I'm not happy. I haven't been happy for a long time. I already told you this." Our voices grew louder as we stood facing off like the many times we had before. The scene in

Dark Night of the Soul

the living room was familiar.

"Kyle, don't you want this marriage?"

"No."

"Then why did you marry me?" I asked.

"I don't know. I shouldn't have married you."

"Then take your shit and get out. Take all your shit. Get the fuck out!"

"No—! I'm not leaving tonight. I'll leave in the morning."

"I want you gone tonight. I can't stay in this place of limbo. If we're not going to be together then file for a divorce. Let's get it over with."

"I'm not filing for a divorce."

"Are you cheating on me?" I had asked Kyle this before and since he left it was a lingering suspicion. My friends squashed the topic when I brought it up but infidelity felt like the only plausible answer.

"Not everyone cheats, Shakirah. Stop being so insecure."

If I knew I was being gaslit and that gaslighting was Kyle's go-to weapon to diminish my esteem, I might have set boundaries. The conflicting part of my faith was being taught to extend forgiveness to those who harm us while protecting myself. I naively believed that God would protect me from Kyle's abuse. I often asked God to keep Kyle away from me as a sign that we were not to get back together. A few days would go pass without hearing from Kyle and I felt ease that I had been freed from my nightmare. But then he would show up as if he hadn't been a terror in our last interaction. He invited me out for dates and I foolishly went along. He drove past our condo and sent me text messages to let me know he was watching me from the window. I took these microaggressions as omens. I lied to myself, believing that God was turning Kyle's heart and if I kept my mouth in check things would get better. They weren't getting better. Our situation was getting worse.

The morning after our blowout, Kyle sent a text to let me know he wasn't returning home. My heart volleyed and scraped my spine as if I had been punched by a poltergeist except the only thing haunting me was Kyle's indecision. There were few reasons to continue fighting for our marriage but I remained steadfast. When Kyle's aggression grew stronger, I prayed harder with a stubborn belief that we were redeemable. I didn't want to let Kyle's abuse convince me that my journey to a life with God was in vain so I protected my hope by no longer sharing where I was in my spiritual journey. I removed every evidence of my life as a Christian — all the scriptures I strategically placed around the condo to commit them to memory were taken down. The faith that remained needed guarding even if my heart was left vulnerable.

***

The weeks following Kyle's return and second immediate exit took a greater emotional toll than I wanted to admit. Prayers I had routinely expressed with fervor became hallowed cries like a kitten in search of its mama. Darkness and depression perched at my bedroom door as hints of an early spring emerged. Getting out of bed was becoming more difficult and the sting of loneliness was baiting me with suicidal thoughts. I struggled to reconcile how I was a Christian who started an invigorating relationship with God yet I was hurting more than ever. My life was supposed to be abundant but things were looking destitute.

Kyle's scent was still on the bed. Each inhale of his lingering scent took me back to moments when we were less volatile. Things between us hadn't always been so bad. At least that's how I comforted myself when intoxicated by

Dark Night of the Soul

the fragrance of him still loitering on his abandoned pillow. I remembered our days laughing at prank phone calls done by radio stations and morning drives to work talking about what our home would be like with children in it. I wanted to go back to make things right between us, but even going back appeared pointless. For seven years, Kyle had been the only constant in my life. If I were going to turn my life around, I wanted Kyle to be there for my victory lap. Besides, it was hard to be angry with Kyle for leaving me when I could find much error in my ways. When I tried to motivate him, he said I was pushing too hard. When I focused on my aspirations he resented me. It was that I hadn't learned the delicate balance of being a wife because I hadn't learned why I married Kyle in the first place. The catalyst of our becoming joined together in matrimony was the best-kept secret between us. A year in and we still hadn't been able to answer Pastor Elliott's question: why marriage to each other?

Of course, I didn't communicate any of this—not my latest bout of depression nor my own uncertainty of our marriage—in our counseling sessions. I convinced Kyle to attend marriage counseling by proposing we use the time to unroot the core issues of our marital discourse. All our truths could be laid bare and we could find resolve at the mercy of a psychologist. I came across Dr. Holloway in a Google search. At the time it seemed important for our therapist to have a set of criteria consisting of three unalienable items. I needed him to be a man —a black man—and Christian. Kyle was reluctant to attend but he showed up to each session promptly. Had he been secretly hoping we could work out too?

Dr. Holloway didn't need too many sessions before diagnosing our issues, the first of which was communication —something I made a note to work on. And second, per the recommendation of our counselor I had to let Kyle vent his frustrations because he was the wronged person (as indicated by his needing to walk out of the marriage). Dr. Holloway said my silence would create a safe atmosphere for Kyle to be completely transparent. Initially, the idea of remaining silent as Kyle berated me with his angry tirades made me nauseated. I had many missteps in our relationship and marriage. Sometimes my ambition took up too much space in our marriage to the point where I could be uncompromising. My unaddressed trauma often made me anxious and my anxiety could turn outward into rage or inward, causing me to shut down. I was anal about the aesthetic of our home. Cleanliness has always been my form of control when everything else around me appeared to be chaotic. I was deeply flawed with no clue how to be Kyle's wife but I could at least express my love for him. Kyle never had to question my devotion to him.

With the little knowledge I had, I worked to make our house feel like a home. And I pushed to know Kyle even when he wanted to remain unknown. I understood that like me, Kyle had been hurt. Hurt people need consistency if nothing else. I agreed to remain silent but I was frustrated that one simple truth would go unexpressed: for as much as I hurt Kyle, he hurt me. Leaving our marriage without giving me (us) the opportunity to correct what was wrong felt selfish. I told myself that with God on my side this time around my forbearance of equivocating on Kyle's marital misdeeds would be vindicated when the time was right. I needed to be patient.

"Do you understand that you are very influential?" Dr. Holloway asked me before Kyle arrived for our bi-weekly counseling session.

"I never considered that … what does that have to do with where we are now?"

"As his wife, it seems your estranged husband is angered

by your words, Mrs. Hardy." He continued.

I hated when Dr. Holloway called us estranged. The way he dragged out each syllable, *es strangg ged*, felt like a knife being jabbed into my heart. I also hated being in Dr. Holloway's old, tiny office. The leather chairs squeaked and the fluorescent lighting did nothing for my depressive state and his office always reeked of mothballs. Sitting in his office was like a being in a reoccurring nightmare. Each week Kyle shared how I tactfully dragged our marriage into a gradual descent with little recognition of how he was complicit. I was too needy, too bossy, and too busy. When asked how I could improve, Kyle would remain silent. Rather than offer insight on how we could come together to revive our partnership, he posited his response as further criticism. Kyle told Dr. Holloway that he didn't need dinner every night or the house always cleaned but he couldn't share what he desired and how we could work together to make our marriage right.

Each week I waited for the answer to drop into my lap like a completed football pass. Oh, how I longed for Kyle to give me any inkling of what I could do to make things better. The answers never came. We continued on in this cycle of Kyle presenting me as a problem through March. Sensing my growing frustration, Dr. Holloway said that breakthroughs took time and that I should remain patient. Prayer, he continued, could change things in a moment's notice. I wanted to tell Dr. Holloway that I had been praying but maybe Kyle was praying too and his prayers were being answered.

On what would be one of our final counseling sessions, Kyle walked into Dr. Holloway's office unphased by my early arrival. He greeted me like he would a stranger in an almost empty Metro train car, polite but detached. I flashed a smile, hoping to warm the atmosphere or at the very least to keep from flying off the handle and beg for Kyle to come home. Following our normal routine, Dr. Holloway started the session with prayer—asking God to give him the wisdom to guide Kyle and me in the way that we should go. Then he went into his usual line of questioning. He asked how our weeks had been going and if we were making progress towards reconciliation. "Fine," Kyle and I mumbled in unison.

When asked why, Kyle went into full mutiny. He repeated all the things that had already been said to me many times before. He was no longer in love. He had no hope for our future and then offered a new revelation. "I think marrying Shakirah was a mistake."

I gave Dr. Holloway a subtle nod to note that I was okay when he looked in my direction. I sat quietly doing my best rendition of a dutiful wife. Kyle also looked in my direction. It was as if everyone in the room expected me to finally implode right then. Because this was Kyle's moment of vulnerability, I gave him the gift of my empathy and support. I stopped considering whether the marriage could be salvageable and started using Kyle's feedback as lamp posts for how I might need to grow. Kyle's words were often harmful. I was suspicious of the validity of what he was saying but because he repeated it so frequently, I had to acknowledge *his* words as his truth. I thought that when Kyle previously expressed regret for marrying that he was reacting out of emotion. When I heard him tell Dr. Holloway that marrying me was a mistake, I knew he meant it. His words were deliberate. He was calm as if he had been considering his actions for a long time. I wondered if on our wedding day he carried those same reservations. It was a sobering reality but I was grateful that we had the truth even if it was half of the truth.

Dr. Holloway was less calm. "You're saying you stood before God, your family, friends, and bride and you didn't mean your wedding vows?"

"That's correct," Kyle said with his face stern.

"So, why did you marry her?" Dr. Holloway asked, still wanting to get at the core of our issues. Kyle looked at me with what could only be described as pity.

"I mean—" Kyle paused as if trying to find the right way to deliver another emotional blow. "I don't want to feel like I keep dropping these bombs on her, but I'm just not in it. I'm not in love with her." Right then was when I made the decision to stop fighting for our marriage.

In our last session with Dr. Holloway, Kyle repeatedly told Dr. Holloway that he didn't want a divorce. Dr. Holloway asked consistently throughout the session to confirm what he was hearing.

"You're saying you don't want to be married but you don't want to file for a divorce?" Dr. Holloway asked.

"That's correct, I don't want to file for a divorce," Kyle said.

"So what are you willing to do, Kyle? How long are you willing to stay in this situation? Your wife wants to be reconciled." Kyle stared at Dr. Holloway like he had done in every session before. The little progress we made was again hindered by Kyle's indecision.

"I offer mediation if you want to consider how to divide your property and assets." Dr. Holloway pushed for Kyle to choose a direction. The new angle of his questioning was less about helping Kyle unpack his feelings and more about getting him to take responsibility and ownership of the marriage even if that meant Kyle would be the one to end the marriage.

"Uh, that won't be necessary," Kyle said.

"Have you all tried dating each other again?" Dr. Holloway

shifted in his seat.

Like me, Dr. Holloway appeared to be running short on solutions. We left the session with the recommendation to stop focusing on the marriage and to start dating each other again. The dating, Dr. Holloway said, was to help us find our way back together. What Dr. Holloway neglected to acknowledge was that Kyle never truly wanted us to be together. Finding my way back to someone who didn't want to be found by me was an exercise in futility. I foolishly agreed to Dr. Holloway's recommendation but committed to myself that I would not initiate a date with Kyle. I would begin the steps of moving on. If Kyle wanted to file for a divorce, I would not stop him but I was out of the ring. There was no more fight for our marriage left in me.

***

Out of our bedroom window, I could see the sun dropping into the earth as the moon started to rise. Against the backdrop of winter, the sky boasted a beautiful purple hue. I turned on one of my new favorite Christian rock singers, Kari Jobe. The words of her songs, borrowed from pages of the Bible, pushed against my depression. Dr. Holloway said depression came from hopelessness. When people are depressed they have lost hope in everything. Spiritually overcoming depression meant finding the will to hope again. There were many circumstances in my life that chipped away at my ability to hope. I could count them like sheep. But, as "The Revelation Song" played, Kari's voice pushed back the depression. The house didn't feel like a battleground anymore. It was calm and peaceful. On my first Valentine's Day alone my home became dance floor where God invited me to join Him. The music, the candles I lit and the gorgeous backdrop of the evening sky postured my soul towards heaven. I knew I still had a long way to go,

Dark Night of the Soul

but I could see the light was coming in. And for once I was being romanced.

Sunday offered relief from the messiness of my marriage. I imagined that attending Holy Gate Church was like walking through the gates of heaven. Week after week I was greeted by constant warmth and openness. I made quick friends with the other young women in my small group and confided in them about the breakdown of my marriage. They agreed to pray with me and said they have faith, God was able to restore anything broken. "His heart is for marriage," they would say while holding my hands in theirs as we bowed in prayer at a moments notice. I was lifted on the wings of their resolve.

These men and women didn't cower at the thought of young husbands walking out on their wives. They didn't show judgment toward a mother who could so easily stop speaking to her child. No. These Jesus-lovers raised their hands to the sky shouting words of praise. They charged God to work in me and in turn work in my circumstances. When they spoke to God they did so with boldness. These people had been in a relationship with God much longer than I. They had established a trust that allowed them to have not only hope but also strong faith that God could do anything. Sunday, a day that I avoided because I knew it meant Kyle dragging me to Mom's humble church, became my favorite day. I longed for the healing balm of Pastor Rubio's sermon. And I felt cradled in safety when surrounded by these young believers.

I attempted to carry the Sunday high with me when I left the church like a kid learns to ride their first training wheels-free bike. I was sloppy and uncertain, but I kept moving forward. There was a new drive in me. Fear still existed. Noori committed to being my disciple. A disciple, I learned, was someone who helped bring a new Christian closer to

Jesus. Once a week we met to talk about the progress of my faith. The start of our meetings almost always consisted of me crying. I was a leaky fountain of tears in church, in small group, and in my discipleship moments with Noori. Confronting my new faith wrung me out like a dirty rag. As I heard about God's love for me, I realized just how little I had been receiving and giving. On the subject of forgiveness, I discovered a wealth of resentments stored in my heart. Faith made a punk out of me because it put me up against myself, my greatest enemy.

***

My college friends were shocked to learn that Kyle and I were separated. I started to tell them one-by-one the details of what happened. On days when the separation became increasingly difficult, they took turns coming to my house to make sure I was okay. When the tears made it challenging for me to talk they lay with me in the bed sharing in my darkness. It was funny; on the one hand, I was finally making amends with the spiritual friction that existed inside of me for so long. And with that, I was learning truths about God, life and myself. On the other hand, my marriage was burning to the ground. The more I tried to save the more the fire stoked. I wanted to find a way to merge the two: my newfound relationship with God and my marriage to Kyle, but they were becoming duplicitous. Kyle was making it clear that he had drawn a line in the sand, a line that left me on the side of darkness. Alone with my God.

***

Chapter Seven

Just Before the Dawn

Nestled under an ominous sky, the atmosphere was quiet—quiet like when the world is gently awakened by the sun. I stood both spectator and protagonist, watching a crowd of people follow me as I walked over a rocky cliff hand-in-hand with a man next to me.

I can't tell you exactly where we were located because our unceremonious precession—the crowd, the mystery man, and me—occurred in the way a movie begins at the middle of the plot. There was a bit of solemn and melancholy in the movement of the people following behind me as we stepped over the crevices of the rocks. As the terrain transformed to flat we moved in silence to another unknown destination. Before I could make any objections to going any further, the man and I entered a cave. Then, without warning, it went dark.

The details of what happened in the cave remain foggy, but on the other side is where the story shifts. We came out of the darkness—the crowd no longer behind us—into a lagoon with the water reaching just above my ankles. I looked down and saw a fish swimming across my feet. Turning to my left, the faceless man and I were still hand-in-hand. I had been holding onto this person whose name I didn't know, nor whose face I could see. He was unrecognizable yet somehow familiar. His acquaintance was like finding a new love whose soul I knew long before he came into my life. "This reminds me of Aruba," I whispered to the stranger.

He didn't respond. Instead, he stood firmly holding my left hand in his right letting his presence fill the silence. As we stared into the distance a wave moved across the water. Only then had it occurred to me that the man never once let me go.

I woke up still feeling the coolness of the lagoon enveloping my small frame as I lay in bed wondering what my dream could mean. I wanted to bottle up the peace I experienced standing with the mystery man and wear it like a sweet fragrance to cover up the stench of bitterness that was growing in my heart. Spring had arrived making it four months since Kyle walked out of our home and I was no closer to answers.

Despite my marriage's gradual descent, my spiritual life was continuing to blossom. I still waxed and waned between the peak of closeness of new believer experiences in a relationship with God, and the pit of the valley — but still, in my pendulum swings, I remained resolved that I could and should believe in God. I retained faith despite Kyle's suggestion that my belief was temporal. Kyle couldn't see the interiority of my spiritual development. Words could not adequately describe to Kyle or anyone what was shifting within my heart. I felt a new kind of strength emerging. Through the years, life had been something I learned to survive. Depression and anxiety were my coping mechanisms. With faith, I developed a new point of reference. Scripture came to me like the lyrics to my favorite song.

Taste and see that the Lord is good.

- Psalm 34:8.

Be anxious for nothing, but in everything, by prayer and petition, with thanksgiving, present your requests to God.

- Philippians 4:6.

I took in a steady diet of worship and prayer. And Noori and I were spending regular time together walking through a discipleship process for new believers. Of the few things I knew about Christianity, discipleship remained an untapped territory. I didn't express it much then but I was grateful that in the middle of planning her wedding, Noori committed so much time to help me rebuild a spiritual foundation. Each week we met up to talk about a different fundamental of the Christian faith using a guide manual. It was like, "How to Be Christian for Dummies" but more flowery. The first week was salvation. "Have you given your life to Jesus?" Noori asked. Her gentle voice invited my vulnerability, beckoning it to a safe place were my truths could be laid bare. "I did," I said. "But, nothing felt different. It just seemed like the right thing to do," I confessed.

Noori had a level of patience I wasn't used to seeing in people. No matter how many questions I asked she answered them with refreshing honesty. In one meeting when we arrived at the chapter on lordship Noori instructed me to read, in my bible, the first book of John. I turned to the book of John and began reciting scriptures. After reading a few lines in my peripheral I could see a confused expression on Noori's face.

"Are you reading the first book of John?" Noori asked.

"Yeah," I said while showing her my bible.

"No," she said, sweetly. "That's *the* book of John. There's also a first book of John." "Well, that's confusing. Why wouldn't they just make a second book of John?"

Noori chuckled when I asked if there were two Johns. We both sat giggling about it for the remainder of my lesson. At the same time I was rediscovering Jesus I was also discovering my laughter.

Kyle's birthday was approaching in April and I decided to plan an evening of dinner and DJing lessons for him. I wanted to show him that even though we were separated I still knew the ways to his heart. While in college he would make mix CDs for me with my favorite songs as Christmas and birthday gifts. The CDs were always labeled with his DJ name, "DJ Such-N-Such." There had been so much tension between us during the previous four months I thought having a fun evening would give us a time to reflect on our marriage, or the possibility of reconciling. I shared my plans with Noori, who agreed that keeping the night lighthearted would give Kyle and me the opportunity to reconnect. Noori—ever the loyal conspirator—helped devise the intricate details of my plan. Logistics were her thing. The big ideas were mine. I outlined a dinner menu comprised of a few of Kyle's favorite dishes. Because Kyle and I weren't speaking regularly and I was trying to maintain peaceful exchanges, I often used email as our means of communication. I sent him an email with an electronic invitation for his birthday. The email indicated that the evening would be a surprise: His job was to arrive at our condo dressed comfortably ready for a good time. He only RSVP'd that he would be there.

Kyle called one week before his birthday asking if there could be a change in plans. He did not offer an explanation as to why he suddenly needed to shift. Though my suspicion peaked, I calmed myself by remembering that in the chasm of estrangement there was little I could demand from Kyle. My logic might not have been the right line of thinking but it was a testament to the nefarious position I found myself in while navigating our murky indecision on the state of our marriage.

I was naturally disappointed but obliged to us having dinner together. All the work put into scheduling his DJing lessons were set aside. Yet I pressed on with optimism that Kyle's birthday could be a turning point for us both. Even when I desperately wanted to stop hanging on, I found a little bit more fight inside. Those days the fight was less for Kyle and more for pressing into the faith that got me out of bed each morning. If I could hold on through the drudgery of our separation — through the uncertainty of where life could take me should we decide not to remain, husband and wife — could there also be hope for our us in despondency?

I spent the afternoon of Kyle's birthday dancing through the kitchen like a Disney princess awaiting her prince. Worship music played as I carefully chopped onions, minced garlic and sautéed a variety of peppers. I mashed the fresh flank of salmon and molded them into patties. As I cooked, I prayed over our household. Prayer became an integral part of my functioning. Prayer was my meditation — my rock and my steady when making it through each day was extremely difficult. Before Kyle left home my greatest problems were completing my grad school assignments and mapping out the next phases of my career. The breakdown of our marriage was presenting me with sets of challenges I wasn't equipped to handle. Prayer served as a tool for managing the pressure. When I talked to God, I asked Him for things—the everyday things. I also used prayer as a way to share fears, concerns, and anxieties I never shared with anyone else before. I prayed for us to enjoy the night celebrating Kyle's latest trip around the sun. I asked God to fill our little house with love; and if it wasn't too big of a request, I asked God to soften my husband's heart towards me again. I wanted to know that he loved me.

When Kyle arrived the atmosphere had been set. Once again I fell into the role of a doting lover. Kyle slipped into the door with a stern look of what I assumed was disappointed. It seemed as though he didn't want to be back home and that his presence was out of obligation. More and more it became clear that Kyle was going through the motions of being a husband. Though physically present, his heart remained wherever he left it before walking through the doors of our condo. Each time he showed up, I imagined Kyle checking off boxes to assuage the guilt he must have felt for abandoning his wife. Perhaps, he told himself that he was doing all he can and maybe that was true but unlike the expectations of my youth, I knew this was the bare minimum. Showing up was the least he could do. Admittedly, I ignored his obvious dismissal of my feelings and my negligence in checking him made me a doormat. It was no wonder Kyle would come and go as he please. I hadn't yet learned to establish boundaries. I traversed on, thinking that my martyrdom was admirable and even desirable.

"Hey," he said, sounding unenthused as he removed his shoes.

"Hi, birthday boy!" I sang trying to hide my lingering pain.

The worship music continued playing in the background as I grabbed Kyle's hand and led him to the dining room.

"Tell me about your day. How is your birthday going?" I asked, gesturing for him to sit at the head of our tiny dinner table.

Kyle sat letting half of his body hang off the chair. I took mental note of what appeared his reluctance to get comfortable. We made it through the first course of the meal with me carrying the bulk of the conversation. Kyle rushed through his meal, keeping his answers to my questions short. What I thought was going to be an evening of rekindling the flames with my estranged husband turned out to be a pit stop. The most substantial part of our evening involved Kyle telling me that he would be celebrating his birthday in Philadelphia the coming weekend.

"Oh, with who?" I asked.

"I'm going by myself." He said.

"Can I come?" I asked, pushing myself to uncomfortable levels of vulnerability.

"No, I said I am going by myself so why would you ask to come." Kyle snapped.

"It just seems strange that you would go alone."

"Well, I've always wanted to go."

I moved to the kitchen preparing Kyle's cake with candles. My stomach felt uneasy at our exchange and I was upset that I had allowed the conversation to get so tense. I was also beginning to feel anxious about how secretive everything seemed to be. As I lit each candle on Kyle's cake I contemplated all the months of confusion I had endured. This is unfair, I told myself. It's unfair to try so hard and get so little in return for my effort.

Before I could bring the cake to the table, Kyle began making his way to the closet to retrieve his shoes.

"You're leaving?" I asked.

"I have family stuff," he said with a slight hesitation in his voice. Kyle's defensive made it clear that there was something else going on.

"Okay — well let me pack up the cake and you can have it with your family," I said.

It didn't matter that I was Kyle's family, too. By now it was clear to me that we were irredeemable. His birthday was the last attempt I committed to making to save us. Without Kyle's participation, there was nothing left for me to do. One person could not salvage our marriage. By the grace of God, I made it through dinner without screaming in a fit of rage. Even though I was sullen, I remained composed. Kyle was putting me through the ringer and he knew it. The harder I worked to improve myself for our marriage the more resistant he became. The more love I showed him, the stronger he became in pushing me away. After Kyle left, I stood in the kitchen with my face clutched into the palm of my hands, thanking God for the hour we shared. My tears were sobering but my heart was grateful.

"Small victories," I said to myself. Small victories.

***

"How did it go?"

I didn't know how to tell Noori that the evening I imagined would be magical turned out to be a complete fail so I tried to avoid the conversation altogether, but she had come to know me well. Spending all of our time together praying, talking about God and sharing our deepest secrets gave us a different kind of intimacy that was new to me. Noori was a friend who cared for my spiritual well-being and that made her compassionate towards anything that could be a hindrance to me finding the peace she learned, from first-hand experience, could come from believing in God.

Noori broached the subject gently and in her gentleness, I bowed to the truth. I told her everything. I told her about Kyle canceling his DJ-ing lessons, his seeming reluctance to stay for dinner, and the worst of it, his supposed solo trip to Philadelphia. And though I didn't say it explicitly, I suspected that Noori was reading between the lines. The resignation in my voice was obvious.

"I'm so sorry, boo," Noori whispered.

"I just don't understand. I'm doing everything I can to save our marriage and it's getting worse."

Noori listened intently as my walls came down. I was reaching my breaking point. The exhaustion, the fighting, and the marriage counseling that proved to be nothing more than an exercise in futility. Trying to save our marriage was wearing on me. I was racking my brain on ways to prove I was an acceptable wife. Kyle's response to what others who I shared our marital problems dubbed as no more than the ebbs and flows of marriage, seemed unreasonable. I will not minimize that I walked into our marriage with a little more baggage than perhaps the average woman. But, I couldn't make sense of how he seemed to turn off like a switch.

In one moment we were planning out the next five years of our lives together: buying a bigger home, doing more traveling and trying for our first child. In the next moment, Kyle was expelling feelings of discontent and resentment that had been bottled for years. I only wanted to make it better, but in working to make it better, Kyle began resenting me even more.

Noori must have grown tired of watching me battle the frustration because she jumped in the middle of my internal dialogue like a referee breaking up a boxing match.

"Maybe you should stop trying," she said.

"What?" I asked.

"Yeah," she said. "Stop trying."

It didn't make sense. If stopped trying to save my marriage

what was going to happen? The thought of packing up my toys, going home, and leaving my crippled marriage on the playground to fend for itself invoked instant panic.

"If you can focus on God, He will take care of your marriage," Noori offered as a solution.

My anxiety moved from panic to anger. This impasse needed to come to an end once and for all. I wanted answers. No matter the direction we decided for ourselves, I wanted to know I wasn't crazy for the haunting sensation of a missing link in the equation. Noori urged me to trust God, an offer I would accept with one concession on His part — answers. Once more I called out for it all to make sense. Why at this moment had Kyle walked away? Why not before we made it down the aisle? Why was he being secretive?

Noori and I were nearing the end of our time working through the discipleship book when we began talking about the ritual of baptism.

"Have you been baptized?" Noori asked moving us on from proselytizing over Kyle. I sat on the carpet adjacent to the bench were I spent many nights knelt on to rest my head as I wept. Noori was seated Indian style atop the bench looking down on me with a glimmer in her eye. Her wedding would be in a few months and she definitely had the bride-to-be glow.

"No," I said still staring at the bench.

"It's something you should consider," Noori said as she shifted the weight of her body.

"Will I have to get dunked in water?" I asked.

"Yes," Noori responded. "But, not for a long time."

"Has anyone drowned being baptized?" I joked, trying to bring levity to the moment. Noori laughed before giving me a primer on water baptism.

"Baptism is your way of showing the world you are Christian— that you're born again. It's also God's way of cleansing us and making us new."

"Have you been baptized?" I asked.

"Yes, but I'm actually considering doing it again"

"That's a whole lot of cleansing, Noori."

Attending Holy Gate as a non-member began feeling inappropriate after some time. It was like being a couch squatter in someone's home. I had joined Noori's small group. I was being discipled and attended church regularly. I had planned to revisit my attendance at Mount Zion's Victory, the church where Kyle's mother was the pastor, once Kyle and I ended our separation. Since our marriage remained on a downward trajectory, I decided it was best to close that chapter of my life.

Noori taught me to pray for God's will on matters that were important to me. God's will, she said, was the direction our lives should truly take if we seek Him and walk obediently. I wanted to be the best possible Christian there could be so I prayed for God's will about everything. *God, is it your will for my marriage to be saved? God, is it your will for me to wear red to work today? God, is it your will for me to be a member of Holy Gates Church?* I looked for signs as an answer to my questions. When I received an email about getting baptized and becoming a church member exactly one hour after saying that last prayer I knew God was telling me to take the plunge. I wasn't going to be a couch squatter any longer. Holy Gates was my new home.

***

Spring was settled by the time I was feeling better after the failed attempt at reconciliation during Kyle's birthday. I stopped taking Kyle's phone calls and was finding my footing as an estranged wife. I hadn't yet decided what I would do about our marriage. Clear answers had yet to come to me. I was reluctant to make any decisions without feeling completely resolved. Since I had done all I could do to repair our breach I wanted to give Kyle the opportunity to do the work if he wanted to try again. I didn't force his hand or initiate steps toward us being back together. I was trusting to God though not for any particular outcome. I was trusting that when the time was right everything would become as clear as I needed it to be.

Marital separation gave me the opportunity to discover new parts of myself and rediscover parts that were hidden under months of depression. Solo trips to the movies reminded me of how much I enjoyed storytelling. Taking myself on dates was a new ritual I promised to keep up no matter my relationship status. I began reconnecting with my close-knit group of college girlfriends, the Chocolate Suite. The Chocolate emerged out of finding a safe community of funny, brilliant and beautiful young black women on a predominantly white college. Having been so scared to answer any questions about how I was feeling or what would come of Kyle and me I retreated away from my social circles. As I came out of my reclusiveness like new spring flowers blooming, my friends surrounded like the warmth of the sun. We planned dinners nights, which allowed me to fall in love with cooking without feeling like I was performing for a man.

After a night of laughing and dinner with the Chocolate Suite, I experienced acceptance. I was accepting myself as flawed because God had accepted me. My friends — new and old— had accepted me. If so many other people could permit the grace to be human, it didn't matter that Kyle was holding me to a different, and dare I say, unfair standard. As I cleaned the kitchen while listening to 90s R&B, Kyle must have sensed that I was letting go. My phone buzzed with an incoming stream of text messages. It was Kyle. He was letting me know that he had been parked outside our condo and was watching me from the windows.

What have you been doing?

Was hanging with the girls, why?

Oh, I was thinking about you so I've been sitting out here. Looks like you were having fun.

Creepy.

LOL. Nah, not creepy. Just missing home. Do you want to grab something to eat?

What do you have in mind?

Jerk Pit?

Actually...I'm going to head to bed. I need to get up early. Thanks for checking in though.

By going out with Kyle that evening, I would be stepping back onto his rollercoaster of indecisiveness. In the months to come Kyle and I would have a few more rounds of our tug-of-war but on that night when the moon was big and the stars were skipping through the sky, I decided to put Shakirah first.

The day of our final discipleship meeting, Noori decided that we should spend our formal time together over brunch in DC. Under normal circumstances, I would have been thrilled by the idea. On that particular Sunday after church, I was overwhelmed with sadness. My marriage was sitting in limbo. Not communicating with Kyle was freeing, just not free enough to fully move on. The fact remained that I was still someone's wife. I was still estranged and I was still unsure of what my future might hold.

Despite my reluctance, Noori and I skipped the quick drive from Chinatown to the city's West End and opted to take the Metro. DC was buzzing with tourists who were either visiting the monuments or getting one final glance at the Cherry Blossoms before they disappeared until the following spring. They filled with the station on what would otherwise be a quiet Sunday afternoon. Noori and I hopped onto the first Red Line train that pulled into the station. Between stops I listened as Noori made small talk with a fellow rider who was sharing that he has missed attending an event at Holy Gates Church. I almost missed that detail because I was looking down ruminating on the ashes that had become my life: my crippled marriage, broken relationship with my mother, mortgage bills and the job I hated had piled on me like a sack of horse manure.

It was the sound of Noori and this stranger's laughter that snapped me out of my zombie-like trance. Still looking down I saw two large feet next to Noori's heels. My eyes moved up his statuesque frame and gazed on his broad smile.

"Oh, this is my friend Shakirah," Noori said, introducing me to her handsome acquaintance. I took his hand into mine giving a gentle shake as he smiled in my direction.

"Nice to meet you, Shakirah."

"Nice to meet you, too."

I continued listening as Noori asked if he would be able to attend Freedom Weekend, a quarterly event our church hosted for individuals looking to overcome spiritual battles. It struck me as off that I hadn't seen Noori's friend in church and was quite surprised he was a member.

"Man — I really wanted to be there but that weekend my family will be in town for my graduation. Guess I'll have to catch the next one."

"Congratulations on graduating. Where did you go to school?" I asked.

"GW." He said looking proud. "It's feeling really good to be done. Those two years were a long stretch." Noori's friend had an accent different from any accent I heard before. It seemed southern but with less of a drawl.

"I got my Masters two years ago so I know the feeling."

Noori, her friend and I continued chatting for the remainder of our short ride to the restaurant. In that limited amount of time, encountering this guy I had met for the first time felt like being reunited with an old friend. There was ease about him— an ease about the way we could talk without missing a beat. Seeing him smile was like drinking homemade lemonade after spending a day in the sun. Being in the presence of a man who wasn't burdening me with his disappointments was refreshing. With everything Kyle told me that I had done to diminish our marriage, I found myself avoiding the company of men. The only exception had been my male best friend, Will, who would swing by the condo to give me pep talks. My esteem was quite shaky and the last thing I considered was the prospect of being romantically involved with anyone outside of Kyle. Speaking to Noori's friend was different. I believe that if time permitted, we could have stood on that dusty metro train talking into eternity.

When Noori and I pulled into our stop at the Dupont Circle station I took one last glance at this gentleman who temporarily rapt my heart. At once my soul knew that man deeply. In some cosmic way, he had always been a part of me.

***

By May Holy Gates' Freedom Weekend came quickly. During Freedom Weekend the church entered a time of corporate fasting that would be followed by two-day workshops used to set members of the congregation free from spiritual bondage. All members of the church would spend three days abstaining from different items we individually selected. During my study time, I learned about fasting. I read that people in the bible used fasting as a means of deepening their connection with God. It was said that as Christians fasting is necessary for our spiritual development. Like all things in my faith, I wanted to be fully immersed in the experience.

The workshops began on a Friday evening. Attendees and members gathered in the basement of a local church to do an in-depth walkthrough of the spiritual principles Noori and I discussed during our discipleship moments. Church leaders lined the hallways with water and fruit for those who were fasting from food. I was growing to love my church family. No matter what the occasion everyone was supportive as evidenced by walking through the hallways; I could see pockets of people I recognized from Sunday services gathered praying for one another. It was not uncommon to hear whimpers and see tears falling from people's eyes as they belted out expressions of gratitude. And then there were pleas for God to heal their loved ones and shouts of joy as some reflected on all He had done. "Hallelujahs" echoed through the corridors of that old, dusty church. Shouts became rally cries of the righteous.

Like many years before when I sat in church with Kyle for the first time, I watched people get up to share their testimonies. Young men and women shared how they overcame alcohol addiction. They talked about letting go of feelings of bitterness after being betrayed by family members. Some shared how God miraculously redeemed areas of their lives that appeared beyond redemption. We were all joined together by our brokenness and because of this, there was no shame in the moment.

I left the church feeling rejuvenated even though day one of Freedom Weekend went late into the night.

My external circumstances were the same by all accounts. On the inside, I was continuing to shift. Never in my life had I seen myself grow so vastly. My responses to difficulties had changed. I was allowing people like Noori and other members of the church into close emotional proximity. I was admitting to myself that getting to the other side of surrender couldn't happen in a vacuum. Healing from years of emotional and sometimes physical trauma didn't need to be a solo endeavor. Though it would take many more years of unlearning before finding who I was always meant to be, I was signed up for the journey.

***

On the second day of Freedom Weekend Noori surprised me by inviting the Chocolate Suite and a few other friends to attend my baptism. When I made the decision to get baptized I didn't tell my friends because I didn't want them to feel like they needed to show up for me. My friends had already done more than enough to support me through my separation. I wanted to take this step as an act of bravery. I'm glad that Noori didn't allow me to experience baptism without them.

As I waited in the pews for my name to be called my friends filed into the seats next to me. One-by-one each member of the Chocolate Suite appeared, greeting me with hugs and gifts to congratulate me for arriving at that moment. My heart was moved by the insurmountable love they showed me. The line of women who previously stood next to me on my wedding day while declaring my vows to Kyle were now standing beside me as I prepared to proclaim my life to Christ. I felt more united to them than I believed I could be to any man. It wasn't always obvious that God was using my girlfriends to be an extension of His love — supreme love. On the day of my baptism, it was clear that these young women were teaching me that love comes in all shapes and sizes and from many backgrounds. And in this way, God had always been present. They were showing me that devotion is possible. Coming into my faith I thought I was going on a journey with just God and me. It turned out that my voyage into a new life wouldn't be one I would take alone.

When it was almost my turn to be baptized I changed into a vintage dress I purchased from a consignment store to hallmark the occasion. The dress would be one that I would keep forever as a token to remember the vow I was making to God. Pastor Darryl, Holy Gates' associate Pastor, walked me to the baptism pool and reminded me of the decision I was making. He also assured me that as he dunked me in the baptism pool I wouldn't drown. I could only suspect this was a joke from Noori.

Pastor Darryl and I stood at the top of the steps behind a curtain that led to the baptism pool. As the congregation continued praying and singing worship song, I peeked out from the curtain to find another surprise from Noori — my mother was also sitting in the church pews. I instantly said a silent prayer thanking God for it all—the pain, the frustration, the hurt—because it all led me to Him.

By the time I ended my prayer Pastor Darryl was reaching for my hand to guide me into the water. The curtains opened and I looked out to see everyone watching in anticipation. Pastor Darryl recited the biblical significance of baptism, reminding everyone that the decision I made was a proclamation to be forever joined together with Christ. He quoted from the book of Colossians: "...*You were placed in the tomb with Christ through baptism. In baptism, you were brought back to life with Christ...*"

"Shakirah, is there anything you want to say to the church before we begin?" Pastor Darryl asked.

"In my 26 years of life, I've done things my way. I've tried to hold onto ideals that haven't served me well. I'm ready to start truly living for God. I'm ready to follow Him once and for all."

I used my left hand to pinch my nose and crossed my right hand over my heart. Pastor Darryl gently pulled my body toward the waves of the pool. Time slowed as the water enveloped me. The same feelings of peace from my dream emerged. Everything was about to change. The Shakirah I once knew would be gone. I closed my eyes as I submerged into the water. Then darkness came just before the dawn.

**

Part III: A New Hope

"We have this hope as an anchor for the soul, firm and secure"

-Hebrews 6:19

Chapter Eight

Let There Be Light

I always wondered about Patsy's indifference to Kyle. When he became a frequent visitor in the Hill household, she never warmed to him the way I assumed most mothers would take to their daughter's boyfriends. Only time enabled her to tolerate his presence. Still, her disinterest was palpable. Patsy rarely asked about the details of our relationship. She never once probed to learn about Kyle intentions or if I had intentions of my own.

There weren't conversations about how Kyle and I would balance the weight of long-distance with the demands and intensity of college. Patsy didn't talk me through what it meant to share feelings with a man or how to navigate the complexity of those feelings.

I often took my mother's passivity to be a remnant of her lingering suspicions of men. Patsy, a woman who had endured many heartbreaks of her own, came from the generation of women who were taught to endure the indiscretions of men silently. So as long as a man did not beat his woman it was permissible for him to hang his hat anywhere that pleased him for the night.

My oldest sister Angeline once told me how Patsy rebuked her for questioning whether she should stay with her husband at the time. Angeline's ex-husband was known for being absent, passive-aggressive and a philanderer. "She told me to go climb into the bed with Darryl and keep my mouth shut," Angeline said. "Can you believe it?"

I could believe it.

Patsy, like many middle-aged black women who had been reduced to being mules for men, learned to gird her pain with hardness. The danger in the imperviousness and hardness that women like my mother exerted was that it made them appear culpable in the missteps of men. I still recall the day my mother's long-term partner, Donald, crashed her car. We had been in Maryland for a few years after leaving New York. Patsy and my father were no longer on speaking terms and she moved on to Donald. Donald didn't have steady employment the way Patsy did. She worked double shifts as a nurse, scraping dollars together to buy a car—her first car in more than 20 years.

Patsy's car was more than a mode of transportation. That black 1993 Mazda was her own piece of liberation. She no longer had to fret over how she would get her two children to doctor's appointments. She didn't need to leave for work two hours before her shift began to arrive on time because she wasn't depending on public transportation.

Donald took that liberation from her when he totaled Patsy's car after using it when she specifically asked him not to drive. I wasn't privy to the conversations Donald and Patsy had behind closed doors. I was too young to have that level of insight. What I could see was Patsy going back to riding the bus each day because Donald never replaced her car. I could also see that Donald was still lying next to my mother in bed each night, unphased and unbothered. Where was her fury?

Patsy expected men to be unfaithful and often argued that no woman should consider herself lucky for finding a good man. Good men did not exist in Patsy's world. If a man started out good it was only a matter of time before he soured like dated milk. Discrediting my mother's feelings was difficult when it seemed she had so much proof. Every man who came into her life had failed her, taking pieces of her softness with him as he left. Her own father was the first culprit.

I should have known Patsy's tepidness toward Kyle was her perceptivity. A woman who has been hurt by a man can sniff out a man with the propensity to hurt. If my mother was aware of what would come of my marriage, I wish she would have warned me. I wish she would have told me that a man who blames his unhappiness on his wife is not a man who should be trusted. I wish she would have told me that a man who cannot make up his mind is more dangerous than a man who breaks your heart outrightly. I wish she would have told me to stay away—pulled me back from Kyle like a mother rushing in to stop her child from touching an open flame.

Maybe she was reticent to stop me from marrying Kyle because she knew I might not have listened. It's more likely that I would have moved further away from Patsy had she encouraged me not to go through with the wedding. Maybe she knew that every woman has to have her heart cracked open by a man she loves too deeply. Maybe she saw the rupture coming and had hoped that because her blood was pumping through my veins I would come out on the other side with a little bit of hardness.

Let There Be Light

***

July tented Maryland with its bombastic heat waves and unforgiving humidity. Kyle and I were still planning to attend Jackson and Noori's wedding together though we were barely speaking. From the moment Kyle left, I had given him seven months to find a resolution. Google searches that led me to discussion boards of abandoned spouses suggested that seven months was not a long time for marital estrangement. Many men and women had waited years for their wives and husbands to return. I gathered from my research that Kyle and I were just getting started on the ride of our marital dysfunction. At the start of my separation from Kyle, I found comfort from those discussion boards. The men and women and I were the heroes of our marriage. We were the glue holding our families together. Our great grandchildren would herald our name.

My internet friends knew of their spouses' unfaithfulness. This seemed to be the only difference between the people I would never meet and me. Their marriage was broken by infidelity. Kyle and I were two young people trying to figure out what makes a marriage work. What escaped me as I read thread after thread on those discussion boards is the pattern of behavior so consistently shared by each of the spouses who fled — even Kyle. The admission of dying love. The blame on the abandoned spouse. The confusion. The secrecy. It was like reading a template and yet I still couldn't see.

By the time July came around, I was annoyed at myself for spending too much time on the discussion boards. I didn't want to be the hero of my marriage. Those people had more patience than me. I was a young woman who wasn't ready for the full-time job of being a long-suffering wife. I deactivated my membership to the discussion board, scheduled an appointment for a new haircut and scribbled one final prayer for my marriage into a journal. *Lord, if Kyle is cheating on me please make it plain and clear. I need closure.*

The answer to my prayer came quickly.

The night before Noori and Jackson's rehearsal dinner was the night before the last day of my three-day fast from food and water. I pushed through the hunger pains with stubborn resolve as if I knew an answer from God would come to me soon. The bed slipped from under me as I hopped to my feet screaming and pushing the giant scorpion off of me. Nightmares were a rare occurrence and yet I could feel the body of the scorpion moving its tail to paralyze me.

The next daytime passed slowly as I waited for a text from Kyle. That evening was Noori and Jackson's rehearsal dinner. I hoped Kyle would ask me to accompany him. When he didn't, I imagined him surrounded by other young married couples who were drowning themselves in love. I pretended that when they asked about his wife he would tell them that I had to work late but he was looking forward to introducing me to everyone at the wedding. I still clung to the taxing hope that he cared for me.

The workday ended an hour early since nonprofits in D.C. often worked summer hours on Fridays. "Shakes — we're going to grab margaritas at Banana Cafe. Wanna come?" A colleague asked just before I slipped out the door. I was on the last day of my fast and was scared to even consider the prospect of food lest God not bring an answer to my question.

When I got back to the condo the air felt different. It was as if there was another person in my company whispering breathlessly into the atmosphere. *Check his email*, a voice prompted me. I paused for a moment considering that I might be delusional from three days without food and water. Before I could bring some reason to the moment, I rushed to the bedroom in search of my laptop. I flung open the computer and furiously typing the first password for Kyle's that came to mind. His first cell phone was a Christmas gift I purchased for him to keep us connected while away at school. The ten digits unlocked all the answers I spent seven months searching to find.

Every day for seven months messages had come from his high school best friend, Natalia. She sent Kyle emails thanking him for the nights they cooked dinner together. I thought back to the many times I begged Kyle to help me in the kitchen. Natalia wanted to know why Kyle would come home to visit me. I thought you don't love her, she wrote sordidly in a message. I don't love her, Kyle said. But she's still my wife. I have to make sure she's okay.

Email was the vehicle that carried Kyle and Natalia's dreams of a life they were building together while I was trying to save Kyle and my life from crumbling. They made plans to attend concerts. Brian McKnight, my favorite artist at the time, was where they discovered their song. A trip to Philadelphia during Kyle's birthday was when Kyle first told Natalia he loved her. They recounted the nights of their intimacy. I was a stumbling block—a hindrance to them moving forward. Kyle didn't give Natalia the answers she wanted when she asked when he was leaving me. Soon he would say. If there was one thing Natalia and I could agree on, it was that soon never came soon enough.

My mind flashed between Natalia and Kyle's email exchanges and the arguments Kyle and I had during our time apart. I felt at ease knowing I wasn't insecure or irrational for demanding answers from my husband. Kyle led me to believe that we were working on our marriage when we weren't. The work Kyle was doing was giving himself an alibi; a way to step quietly into his new relationship if I were the one to officially call our marriage quits. Kyle didn't want our marriage to be saved. He wanted to alleviate himself of the guilt of ending it before it had time to ripen.

I continued scrolling through his emails to the beginning of our marriage to find the spark that initiated this wildfire. Eight months after our wedding Kyle messaged Natalia inviting her to a baseball game. The invitation to the game was never mentioned to me.

Natalia had been a visitor in our home many times. I greeted her at our door during the holidays with a warm smile and a sisterly hug. When it was her birthday each November, Kyle insisted we swing by her house to celebrate. I trusted that no matter what difficulties could befall us, infidelity would not be one because Kyle knew more intimately than any other person in my life how betrayal destroyed my family. Fidelity was my only request.

Kyle was at Jackson and Noori's rehearsal dinner when I called him.

"Why, Kyle?" I asked the moment he answered the phone.

"Why what?"

"Why couldn't you just tell me there was someone else? I asked you and you told me I was being insecure."

Kyle was silent on the other end. A minute passed before I could hear him making his way outside of the restaurant.

"How did you find out?" He asked.

"I checked your emails."

"Shakirah, why are you checking my emails?" His tone was angry and I detected a hint of indignation.

"Kyle, I think it's best that you stop contacting me," I said just before hanging up the phone.

The walk from my bedroom to the living room felt like a prisoner taking her final steps on death row. At the peak of day, light normally flooded the condo because the days were longer yet I don't recall the warmth or brightness of the sun. My body trembled while I sat thinking about what was confirmed. The signs had been there so I found solace in knowing my feelings were not paranoia. I was not insecure as Kyle suggested.

Pictures of Kyle and I occupied every space my eyes met with each slow and daunting step I took. I tried to cry but the revelation of another woman loving my husband sapped my remaining strength. If there were accurate words to describe how hurt I was, I would've prayed. Yet, nothing could earnestly convey to God how Kyle's betrayal and blatant disregard for my heart gutted me. My phone buzzed repeatedly and I knew it was Kyle calling out of shock I had actually discovered what was happening. He had no more leverage over me. Kyle and I built our marriage on a house of cards and the walls came tumbling down. After hitting the decline button on Kyle's fifth repeated attempt to call me I paced the living room thinking of what my next move would be. I was calm yet frantic like a duck on water. I was sad yet vindicated. I was burdened by the weight of having to decide how I would respond; yet freed from feeling like an insane person.

For seven months I worked doggedly to prove to Kyle I was worthy of being his wife and that our love deserved his fight. My apologies were relentless and I cowered in our counseling sessions when Kyle told me quite frankly I was a mistake. I was relieved to know that solely my being the world's worst wife did not mark Kyle's leaving. I was, however, humiliated by my foolishness. Kyle and I didn't have the strongest relationship, but I trusted him with my life. I trusted that he would have used one of the moments in our months of marital counseling, to tell the truth. I trusted that he would have been noble enough not to take advantage of my vulnerability and desperation to save our marriage. The estranged dates, the counseling sessions, the physical intimacy were all exercises in futility because while I was working my ass off to become better for him, Kyle was giving his heart to another woman. He took away my ability to make an informed decision on how to navigate our marital dysfunction and let me run on a hamster wheel of his lies and deception. He placed me in a race without letting me know I was competing, or that I had already lost before I could even start.

I wanted to be infuriated, but the sadness was too heavy so I sat on the couch scrolling through my phone book searching for someone to call. Between ignoring more of Kyle's calls I managed to get my college girlfriends on the line. We developed a friendship to withstand moments like this and even though we were two years fresh out of college — too young to have any indication on how to address marital infidelity — I needed them by my side. My Chocolate Suite girls didn't hesitate to come to be with me when I sent a group text telling them what I discovered.

"I don't think you should go to the wedding," Lacy said as she got up to make a cup of tea.

Kyle and I were scheduled to attend Jackson and Noori's wedding taking place the next day. I was to attend as a guest while Kyle served as one of Jackson's groomsmen. Our RSVP card read that Mr. and Mrs. Hardy would be delighted to attend the nuptials of Jackson Garcia and Noori Jones. The dress I planned to wear was initially picked—I knew Kyle would like the way it hugged my frame. When I purchased it, I envisioned Kyle seeing me from across the dance floor and thinking to himself how foolish he was to leave. Our eyes would meet and we would fall in love—real, unbreakable love. Now all I could envision were the emails. Months worth of trip planning, sneaking around, love confessing, Shakirah–bashing emails.

Let There Be Light

"I have to be there, tomorrow isn't about me," I said looking at my friend's solemn faces.

There was pity in their eyes, a look I had grown accustomed to over the last seven months as friends listen to me speak in faith that God would restore my marriage. But I still needed to be at the wedding. A small part of me hoped it could be one last ditch effort for Kyle to come to his senses. Maybe, I thought, he would still look across the room and see there was something valuable and salvageable between us. And a larger part of me owed so much to Noori. I knew from my own experience the great undertaking of planning a wedding. Noor did not use wedding planning as an excuse for not being available to support my spiritual development.

In my young adult life, I had been introduced to many different gods. From a brief encounter at a Baptist church when I was 10, I met the Pentecostal God who blessed people with full bank accounts. In Kyle's church, I met the god who stared down on humanity intently waiting for us to get caught in the act of sin so He could quickly banish us to hell. And in my own mind, I wrestled with the perception of a cruel god who allowed families to be torn apart and havoc to be wreaked on the earth. None of these were the God Noori and the rest of the Holy Gates Church community allowed me to meet. Through them, I encountered the true God who forgives sins, who mends broken hearts and makes us new. Sharing in her wedding day was only one small way to express gratitude for all she had done.

"But, are you going to be okay when you see him?" Starria followed up.

"I will be okay," I said letting a flood of tears roll down my face.

I wasn't sure that I would be okay, but pushing through adversity is the only way I knew how to survive. All I had to do was make it through a few hours.

Until My Surrender: A Story of Loss, Love and Letting Go

After the girls left I went back to my computer to read through Kyle's emails one more time. Before I could put myself through any more torture, Kyle changed the password. He hadn't made it home to apologize. He did, however, have the gumption to continue covering his tracks. I closed my laptop and did the one thing I had become very good at. I talked to God. "Lord, before Kyle and I got married I asked you if he was the one. I guess my asking was an indication he wasn't. Thank you for shedding light on what was happening. I'm not sure what happens next but this is where I stop. I can't fight for him anymore. I don't have anything left in me."

***

Kyle's phone calls and text messages continued until the morning of Noori and Jackson wedding. I woke with a headache so intense it felt like someone hit me with a sledgehammer the night before. I briefly assumed the night before was a bad dream until I received a flood of text messages from my friends telling me to rethink attending the wedding.

While preparing for the wedding I oscillated between my options. I could keep fighting like the spouse who I met on the discussion boards. Those who were fighting to repair their marriage after and in the midst of infidelity were fighting with one hand behind their backs and they often couldn't see their opponent. When someone chooses to love another person outside of their committed relationship, they often make the spouse the enemy. The spouse who is left to hang on doesn't always see the ways the other person is setting themselves up to win by playing into the cheating spouses insecurities.

The other option was to leave; to evade hardness, preserve my softness by walking away. To silence the noises I told

God that if He could promise to be with me, I would make it through the day in a way that would honor Him. Worship music filled the house as I dressed for Jackson and Noori's big day. July in Maryland usually came with an influx of humidity, but the weather was mild enough for me to open the windows and let in the steady breeze. Once donned in my dressed I looked in the mirror to see a tiny woman staring back at me. My collarbone protruded more noticeable than usual and my frame was smaller, a lot smaller than it had been since high school. Still, I forced a smile, reminding God of a previous joke we shared. "God, does the offer for that tall, handsome man still stand?" My wedding ring glimmered in the mirror's reflection. After debating whether to wear it I decided to keep it on as a means of saving face from questions that would surely follow my not wearing it.

A mutual high school friend of Jackson and me offered a ride to the wedding. I told her Kyle was a groomsman and needed to be at the venue much sooner than me and I wasn't keen out waiting around outside for hours before the ceremony started. While my excuse worked to get me a ride it did not keep us from arriving 20 minutes behind schedule. Fortunately, the ceremony hadn't yet begun. We showed up in Baltimore to the beautiful courtyard blanketed in yellow and grey decorations. Large pom poms hung from tree branches and white-folding chairs covered the grassy area just before the gazebo where Jackson and Noori would say their wedding vows. We seated ourselves in one of the last rows of the groom's side where only three remaining seats were open. My newly established date's dress zipper under her left arm got snagged, forcing us to sit in the two seats at the end of the aisle. Instrumentals of contemporary Christian music played while guest mingled, waiting in anticipation for the ceremony to begin.

I searched the landscape to see if I would see Kyle.

"If I stay here everyone is going to see my side boob. I'm going to move to that seat down there." She said pointing to the remaining empty chair to my right.

"Okay," I said, helping her move in between the narrow row of chairs while still trying to spot Kyle.

The music softened as Pastor Rubio asked remaining guests to take their seats. In my peripheral was a tall shadow inching nearer to me. I looked up to see a face I recognized.

"Is someone sitting here?" He asked already planning to sit.

"No," I said shocked to see him at the wedding. Instead of asking what he was doing at Jackson and Noori's wedding I decided to make small talk, hoping the answer would emerge naturally. I could only remember a few details from our previous conversation and unfortunately one of those details was not his name.

"How's life after graduation?" I asked while he adjusted his long limbs between the unforgiving rows. Looking straight into my eyes he flashed a smile, the same smile that made him feel like a long time friend the first time we met.

"Ah man, it's good. It's real good. I finally have some free time for myself, ya know?" His accent was heavy and distinct I still couldn't place it.

All I knew was everything he said was charming. His demeanor was so warm it invited me back to the space where I tried to pinpoint how a complete stranger could capture my attention.

"So who'd you come here with?" He asked.

I didn't want to tell him that 24 hours before the wedding I found out my husband was having an affair and in a few minutes, he would be standing at the altar while his best friend got married. That nugget of information seemed inappropriate for the mood. So I introduced him to my pseudo date who was still fiddling with her defective zipper. Why she hadn't given up on that thing was beyond me, but I admired her determination.

"Oh, I'm here with my friend Tammy. She and I went to high school with Jackson." I said pointing at Tammy.

Hearing her name brought Tammy back to the wedding and out of her zipper, fixated daze. She paid no mind to the fact that a very handsome man was seated next to me. For all she was concerned he was just another wedding guest.

"Tammy this is—" "Sam," he said, reaching his hand out to Tammy. "I'm Sam. Nice to meet you, Tammy."

Sam and I didn't talk about having been introduced to each other by Noori on the train three months before the wedding. We fell into conversation with a natural flow, laughing and telling stories about our iPhones. We were fast new friends whose souls obviously had a long history before we came into creation. I did learn that Jackson was for Sam what Noori had been to me. Jackson was Sam's disciple and in that time they developed a close friendship. It made sense. Jackson was the kind of man who could make friends with anyone. His heart was boundless in a way that welcomed everyone in. And Sam struck me as a man with a similar heart. I imagined their friendship with as much depth as Jonathan and King David who I learned about reading the bible. In our conversation, Sam told me how he worked in healthcare and his previous job working for a pharmaceutical company required frequent trips to Baltimore.

"Getting here was no problem. I know 395 like the back of my hand." He joked.

The music grew louder queuing the ceremony was about to begin. Out came Kyle as the groomsmen lined the gazebo.

I expected him to show up worn and tired from crying his eyes out the night before. No such evidence presented itself. In fact, Kyle looked great. No matter much how of a jerk he could be, there was no taking away from how handsome he was. I tried to see if he was looking for me in the ocean of wedding guests. He looked straight ahead as if trying to keep his focus. I looked down at my wedding ring and wondered if Sam had noticed it. Guilt crept into my heart as I contemplated taking it off. Kyle was never going to love me, I thought to myself. Why did I even bother to try? I twisted the diamond on my engagement ring. I glanced over at Sam who was watching his friend Jackson wait for his bride.

When Noori walked down the aisle it was like God used the sun as a spotlight to shine on her. She was the epitome of a blushing bride. Jackson, like the rest of us, could not hold back our tears in the face of her beauty. Their eyes locked as she moved towards her new future. When Noori took her position next to Jackson, Pastor Rubio asked the congregation to bow our heads in prayer. Immediately and instinctively I took Sam's hand into my own as Pastor Rubio began to bless the couple.

"He who finds a wife finds a good thing." Pastor Rubio said, quoting from the Book of Proverbs. I don't know if it was God or my own crazy thoughts but a small voice whispered, "Sam has found his wife."

* * *

By the time we made it to the reception, it didn't matter that my fantasy of Kyle falling in love with me from across the dance floor had been deflated. Watching Jackson and Noori stand together throughout the night, and stealing glances at Sam cemented what I had always been too afraid to accept. Kyle was right, us getting married was a mistake.

Let There Be Light

As I watched Jackson stand by Noori's side beaming with pride throughout their wedding night, I came into the realization that Kyle and I could never have that kind of marriage. The signs I had been seeking repeatedly slapped me in the face. The revelation of Kyle's affair was the sign that fell into my lap. I could no longer ignore the dysfunction of our marriage.

I couldn't see a path to reconciliation that could manufacture the kind of love I desired. I wanted closeness, true closeness rooted in intimacy. Kyle and I would never be that close. While watching Jackson and Noori dance the night away, whispering loving words into the atmosphere I decided I needed to let my marriage go. My marriage to Kyle represented the two decades of wreckage I carried with me. I walked into a matrimony built on an obligation. My brokenness was present enough that Kyle felt obligated to marry me. Not only did I decide to let my marriage go, but I decided to also work on releasing everything that represented a life riddled with reacting to the symptoms and triggers of my trauma. I decided to let go of the pain.

***

The next day at church was membership inductions and I would be welcomed into the Holy Gates Church spiritual family. The problem was the sentiment of the wedding wore off. Somehow I managed to make it to service looking half decent while feeling like an 18-wheeler had run over my heart. I arrived at the theater early and was greeted by Sam who was, shockingly, an usher. In all my time attending Holy Gates, I had never seen him—not in passing between services or being ushered to my seat. If I didn't know any better I would have believed he dropped out of the sky. And Sam was the kind of man who appeared to never have a bad day because at 8 o'clock on Sunday morning his megawatt smile was putting the sun out of business.

As much as I was happy to see him I wanted to avoid making small talk. The reality that I would be filing for a divorce on Monday made my body ache. I wasn't wearing my wedding ring and still couldn't ascertain whether Sam knew I was married and was the overly friendly type. Maybe he was exhibiting southern hospitality. Or if not, was he showing interest? I was too fragile to give any of it too much thought.

"Hey! Good seeing you." Sam said sounding delighted by our third serendipitous encounter. My second order of business after filing my divorce papers was figuring out where his accent originated.

"Good morning." I sang. I was trying to hide my agony and hoped Sam wouldn't ask if anything was wrong.

"How long did you stay at the wedding?" He asked.

"I stayed the whole time. I couldn't miss the Electric Slide." Throwing in jokes was sure to evade any suspicions of my pending breakdown.

We made small talk about how the rest of the evening went before I took to my seat.

"Enjoy the service," Sam said before returning to his post at the front of the theater's entrance.

Standing at the front of the church to be inducted as a member signified another major step in my spiritual journey. While I was losing one family, I was gaining another. It was interesting that at the crossroads of my spiritual development a core component of my life was being knocked from under me. In the New Testament, Jesus tells His first disciple that in order to follow Him they needed to leave everything, including people they loved behind. One way I interpreted Jesus' instruction was an encouragement to let go.

I don't think Jesus' intention was to undermine the value of the possessions and the people the disciples would be leaving, but I sense Jesus knew that for each disciple they were holding on to things that would keep them from moving freely through the adventure of knowing Christ. And for me, God knew my marriage to Kyle was another shackle. I don't blame Kyle for the person I was in our marriage. We both had our share of faults, but someone had to be the one to confront the truth. I wasn't going to stay on the hamster wheel or seek revenge by cheating, too. Nothing good would come from me reacting out of spite. Kyle and I were too young to know what it was to love. And we could have made it, but his heart was never there and it was never going to be. The choice to divorce Kyle was the choice to keep moving toward freedom.

One week after the wedding Kyle came to remove his belongings from our condo. Until then he didn't know I filed for divorce. As he packed his boxes I wanted to give it one last shot. It was my Hail Mary pass to see make sure I wasn't being unreasonable.

"Kyle, I just want to know why?" I asked as I watched him toss shoes into a U-Haul cardboard box.

"You think us being separated has something to do with me cheating. It doesn't."

"But why, Kyle? Why didn't you tell me?"

"Look, Shakirah. The only reason why I stayed with you for so long is that I just didn't want to be another person in your life who hurt you." That was the final punch.

On Kyle's way to the door, I told him I filed for a divorce. He stopped to take a good look at me before letting the door slam.

***

Chapter Nine

Broken Mirrors and Old Wineskins

I've heard people say that the loss of a marriage can be equated to the death of a loved one. The analogy seemed hyperbolic until I experienced my own. It's true—death and divorce are synonymous, in a way.

There are many painful things you have to deal with when dissolving your marriage: deciding who gets the house, choosing whether to keep your married name, alerting your family and friends, telling your kids (if you have any) and of course losing someone you love. But the most painful thing so rarely discussed is the divorce hearing and all that follows. If your wedding day is the peak of birthing a new love, then the divorce hearing is its antithesis. It is the day you lay the vows you declared, the dreams you hoped to manifest, and the plans you made to rest.

On the morning of my divorce hearing, I dressed in all

black—prepared for a funeral of sorts—and made my way across the county to the courthouse, the same courthouse where Kyle applied for our marriage license. The long and lonely drive was a procession of anxiety. I couldn't help feel as though I were betraying my soon-to-be ex-husband. When you are married there is an unspoken commitment to protect the intricacies of your matrimony. You tuck away any offenses and lie about being happy. You put on fake smiles and you do not, under any circumstances, tell people that you are miserable. That unspoken commitment is forsaken when you stand before a judge baring the nakedness of your spouse's indiscretions. Exactly one year after Kyle walked out of our home we stood before a judge who declared us no longer married. And like with death, I would need to begin the long road to healing and acceptance of a life that would no longer be.

In the months leading to our hearing, I ceased all contact with Kyle and made efforts to work on healing. For a time it was going well. The quiet space of my new life as a single person I found greater depth in my relating to God. I followed the biblical example of Ruth who was blindly loyal in her commitment to a faith that was not her own. My life was still not making any more sense than it did nine months before I trusted God was leveling out my path. And that trust, even when it was shaky trust, kept me holding on to God. I couldn't see then what God was doing, which was painful when I considered what it meant not to have prayers answered coupled with the lack of resolve from my broken relationship with my mother and my father's death. What was undeniable was Pastor Rubio's words and the people who, since building a new spiritual foundation, had come into my life. In their own way each person was a post sign. Noori, Pastor Rubio and his wife Mrs. Grace, the new friends I made at Holy Gates Church. And Sam.

I had fallen in love with Sam. We existed in a state of bliss reveling in the holy providence God orchestrated. When Sam came into my life I found a new heartbeat. After the wedding, regularly seeing each other in church or at church events gave Sam and me moments to get to know each other and build a friendship.

We shared smiles over hopes for great adventures in our newfound spiritual place. The more I learned of Sam, whether through our interactions or word of mouth, the fonder I grew of him. I was also cautious. I wasn't so naïve as to not recognize the vulnerable position I was in. I had come out of a nine-year relationship and marriage to a man who betrayed my heart. As best as I could muster up, I tried to find reasons not to like him. I tried to coax myself into putting up stronger boundaries but I didn't want to. We didn't plan for love to happen—no one ever does—but we weren't prepared to stop it. Not immediately.

Our rapidly budding friendship was becoming evidently romantic. Sam was the only man in our church I hugged and had given my personal cell phone number. He used it twice: once to wish me a Merry Christmas and once to invite me to coffee so we could have a talk. Our talk is what set us on a new course.

A month after my divorce finalized Sam and I met in Lafayette Park outside the White House. Thanks to global warming and the graciousness of God it was unseasonably warm for February. In our phone conversations, Sam was vague about the details of what our talk was to be about. By then I was in love, which made me anticipate that our conversation would be his gently letting me down. On my walk to the park from the Metro station, I imagined Sam telling me how sweet I was, how much he appreciated my friendship but he saw me as nothing more than a sister because no one meets the love of their life while going through a messy divorce.

We sat on the park bench making nervous small talk before I broke the cordiality.

"What is it that you want to talk about?" I asked.

Two squirrels were playing in front of us. I assumed one was male and the other female because they chased each other the same way Sam and I had been trying to figure out what was happening between us.

"You really get to the point, huh?" He said, adjusting himself.

I looked over to see Sam's leg fidgeting and him brushing his hands against his jeans like he was wiping them clean. His forehead was shiner than normal. It was warm for February but not hot enough for either of us to be sweating.

Sam was nervous. "I just wanted us to get together to clear the air."

There it was, the words I was dreading.

"About what?" I said, trying to hide my disappointment.

"Well, I've been hearing things."

"Like what things?" I asked. My blood was beginning to bubble like a brook. The conversation was taking an unexpected turn.

"I heard you like me?" It was time to come clean and put a swift end to my hopes of us running off into happily ever after.

"I do like you, Sam. I think you're a great guy and I'm not ashamed to tell you that I like you as more than a friend."

"That's a relief to hear because I like you too, Shakirah."

That's where we started, on a park bench in front of the White House on a warm February day. We were inseparable and for a time I forgot I was a woman with a failed marriage under my belt until Sam told me he wanted to marry me.

He dropped hints before fully confessing. There was the day he mentioned wanting to buy a house in LeDroit Park and asked me what I thought of the neighborhood. Or, the time he told me he wanted me to be with him when he bought his first dog, a dog he would name Marley after my favorite musician Bob Marley. Sam talked about the future a lot and somehow he always managed to write me into it. The crazy thing is, I could picture it. I could see us old and in love sitting on the porch of our wraparound deck drinking lemonade while laughing at how we met three times. But when Sam told me he wanted to marry me after our public date as an official couple, I froze because all I could remember was how horrible I was in marriage. And when I remembered that I asked how was it possible for a man as tender and loving as Sam to want to share his life with me?

Sam told me he would be patient while my heart healed. Of the many things, we shared in common, broken hearts was one. A year before I met Sam he walked away from a tumultuous relationship with a woman he thought he had wanted to marry.

"I put more love into it than she was willing to give," he told me over dinner one evening.

Sam was my mirror. When I looked at him I could see the small bits of goodness I had within myself, like my willingness to seek love at all cost. We were both passionate and idealistic. We were both also deeply afraid of making the same mistakes again. Still, the fear didn't stop us from trying. We were intentional about doing things differently than we each had done in the past. And for the both of us that was keeping God central to our foundation building. Sam shared his journey to God; his journey paralleled mine though we didn't have the same upbringing. When Sam told me that God designed his heart to love me and that our life's circumstances were orchestrated to lead us together I remembered Pastor's Elliott's words, marriage is intended to glorify God. Sam led us in prayer each time we got together and he never stopped reminding me that I was his special gift sent from heaven. He didn't stop at words; Sam's actions echoed his feelings.

"I got invited to my friend's wedding in May. It will be in Charlottesville. Ever been?" We were sitting in Sam's new apartment planning our weekend.

We quickly developed little routines together. Sam knew I was selling my condo and offered up his place as my second home. We were adamant about waiting for marriage before engaging in physical intimacy so weekends at Sam's place meant crashing on the sofa bed, watching Redbox DVDs until we fell asleep.

"Oh, that's nice," I said letting my voice carry from the living room to Sam's bedroom.

"I was thinking you could be my date." I didn't respond immediately because I wanted to temper my excitement. The silence brought Sam to the living room where I was seated Indian style on the couch I had come to love.

"Did you hear me? I want you to be my date."

"Does this mean we get to dance together?" I asked.

"Because dancing is my favorite thing in the world." I enjoyed finding different ways to make Sam laugh.

Dancing was my favorite thing to do, and following that was being Sam's delight. I didn't need to tell Sam it would be an honor to be his date. He could see it in my eyes. He saw everything in my eyes, my joy, my fears, and my insecurities. None of it scared him away, though I was certain one-day it would. For two people who both knew heartbreak, we weren't afraid to look each other in the eyes.

My friends, Noori included, cautioned me that while Sam sounded like an amazing man things seemed to be moving too fast too soon.

"How can you put a time on love?" I asked Noori during another one of our girl-talk sessions. My one-to-one sessions with Noori graduated into a friendship, a boo-ship, as we liked to affectionately call it.

"I'm not questioning the love you and Sam have for one another, but I do wonder if this is the season?"

Season was another one of those Christian buzzwords I was learning. It meant that God orchestrated the events of our lives in segmented flows. God's seasons don't occur like normal seasons. His spring doesn't always immediately follow winter. And the duration of a season isn't relegated to the timing of months. But every time Sam and I came together it was hard to imagine that we weren't in the appropriate season for our love.

"I don't know, Noor. I'm following my heart on this one. This feels different." Noori didn't offer a counter-argument. She told me she supported whatever decision I made. I knew she wasn't against our relationship but the rapidness of it made her uneasy. Like Sam and I, she agreed to remain in prayer about how God would direct us to move forward.

Forward is where we went, our new love marching in with the spring. I sat across from Sam at one of his favorite coffee shops in the City. He made sure we came on a Saturday for Bob Marley night. Sam wanted me to hear my favorite songs being played as he made himself more vulnerable to me. The small coffee shop that doubles as a lounge in the evenings was bustling with young hipsters from around the country. DC is a city known for drawing transplants from everywhere. We sipped wine while I sang along to classic Bob Marley songs. A lone candle softened Sam's structured face. He was letting his beard grow and a hint of a five o'clock shadow was emerging. It was a far cry from his usual buttoned up and polished look but I liked seeing him that way, relaxed and enjoying the moment. He told me stories of life growing up in Detroit and was impressed by my knowledge of Motown.

Mid-way through our conversation Sam stopped.

"I need to ask you something," he said. He picked up his glass of wine, gave it a swirl and placed it back on the table. His body leaned in closer as if he was readying to tell me a secret.

"I'm a little afraid to ask this because I'm not sure how you'll answer but here it goes—"

"What is it?"

"If I asked you to marry me tomorrow what would you say?" I played coy a bit looking away before looking directly into Sam's eyes.

"I would be delighted " I said before sipping more wine.

We began framing our conversations around how life would play out as a married couple. I enjoyed the conversations and the thought of spending my life with Sam, but the anxiety re-surfaced. It surprised me to see how affected I was by Sam's intention to make me his wife. It's what I wanted. Sam was a dream, but I didn't trust myself to maintain his heart. Sam couldn't see the signs of my depression creeping back in right away and if he did, he never said much. Some days I would become completely silent and get lost in a trail of my own thoughts. When Sam wasn't around Depression would show up again and this time around Fear was Depression's faithful sidekick. Those two taunted me with visions of being abandoned yet again. Sam doesn't really love you, they would say. Who could love a woman like you? I believed their words to the point that I began repeating them. Out of the blue, I would ask

Sam if he was sure he wanted to marry me. He handled the question with ease until it became frequent and various in its form. Then I started to see through our prayer time that Sam began questioning, too.

I had high highs and disparaging lows since the M-word was formally introduced into our relationship. Everything was a trigger, especially the topic of family. When he asked about my relationship with my mother I got angry that somehow my dysfunction was still trailing me.

"Would you want to invite her to our wedding?" Sam asked during our routine nightly phone calls.

"No, babe. I don't want her there and even if I did I don't think she would come." Sam began keying in on my pressure points. In his love for me, he gently encouraged me to reach out to my mother. He said it was an area that I would need to address at some point and given the death of my father I shouldn't allow my relationship with my mother to die, too.

Bringing baggage into our relationship was inevitable. All the things I hadn't handed to God I dropped at Sam's doorstep. I cast Sam in the shadow of Kyle's mistakes and I legitimized myself as unworthy of being loved even though God through Sam was telling me otherwise. By Easter Sam had found me curled up on his bathroom floor four times as a result of nervous breakdowns. I unraveled before his eyes, shrinking back into the clutches of darkness. He was trying to save me, but I was hypersensitive and mistrusting. I didn't speak up in moments when my voice was important, and I neglected my healing process for the sake of trying to be formidable for Sam. He was pouring love into old wineskins. It was leaking out of every crevice of my still, unhealed heart. I was locked inside myself screaming that I just wanted to be free. I just wanted to be free. *I just want to be free* is what I would pray to God when I needed to understand how it was possible to meet Sam but be so unprepared to be loved by him.

God was there in the un-timeliness of our romance. He was there in our prayers waiting for the right moment to course correct, waiting until we both had seen just how bad it was for me. Sam would get on his knees and ask God to mend my heart. When I was hurting it was clear he was aching from my sadness. And I believe if there were more he could have done, he would have tried.

***

My bible opened to Galatians 5:1, "It is for freedom Christ has set you free. Stand firm then and do not let yourselves be burdened by a yoke of slavery." I was going through a 40-day fast with my church to prepare for the forthcoming holiday season. Sam was on his way to my apartment. My heart was heavy because I knew what was about to take place. We were eight months into our relationship and two weeks before our marriage preparation classes were scheduled to begin. Sam had been distant since he registered us for the class. When he suggested we have a talk, I knew it wasn't going to be like the talk that brought us together eight months before. My downward spiral into depression hadn't gotten any better. I knew his patience was waning.

I opened the door to see his clean-shaven face solemn. Rarely did Sam appear sad but that evening his melancholy was apparent. As we sat on the couch Sam went on to tell me how much I mean to him, how deep his love for me has grown but he didn't know how to fix it anymore. "You need to heal" were the only words that came through clearly enough for them to stick. He held my hand as we cried together. Sam was right, there was nothing left for him to do. I remembered one day during a drive to North Carolina Sam told me he had a dream we were on a boat in the middle of the East River. Sam said he was paddling so hard to get us to the other side but the boat sat in the river unmoved.

The weeks following our breakup were the standard—awkward and emotionally charged. Sam and I tried to figure out if this breakup was truly the end of us. I made attempts at convincing him we could make it work by suggesting we move forward with pre-marital counseling. It was a desperate and foolish move but I didn't want to risk losing him altogether.

Sam was resolved in his decision and already put up strong emotional walls. His phone calls and emails stopped abruptly. We grew distant out of a need to protect one another. In time I stopped seeing Sam in church and had heard from a mutual friend he moved back to Detroit. I was devastated at the thought that something so full of promise could die so quickly. My natural inclination was to continue holding on —to wait out the shock and believe that we would find our way back together.

I entertained my naivete and sat with the unfounded belief that Sam and I could create a marriage built on my brokenness and his inability to handle a woman so fragile. It would be the second time I expected a man to fix me. My uncertainty passed when I remembered what Noori had taught. Everything comes in seasons.

***

Chapter Ten

Food, Forgiveness and the Five Love Languages

S am was gone and I had a decision to make. I could treat this heartbreak like every other unfortunate event in my life by falling victim to it, or I could learn to grow through the pain. Neither choice was desirable if Sam wasn't apart of the equation. Going through a divorce with Kyle was painful. But, losing Sam knocked the wind out of me. When he walked out of the door of my tiny condo—I saw all of my dreams leave with him.

I wanted to believe that we shared something deeper. You know the old proverb; some people are in our lives for reasons and some for seasons. I didn't want Sam to be a lesson because losing his friendship and love carried a hefty price tag. Yet, I couldn't ignore his words to me during our break up conversation. *You need to heal* echoed in my mind when I sat in the darkness of my bedroom too numb to cry. His words pointed me to the itemized list of hurts I buried under the bosom of my soul. Kyle once told me I always played the victim, a stinging and punctuated truth made evident by my pushing Sam to the edge of his comfort zone. I was a victim carrying grievances, regrets, fears, and resentments towards the people who hurt me and quite frankly towards myself. And this victimization marred the new Shakirah that God was calling me to be.

Now I was alone—really alone—to face this great Love that spent the last 28 years pursuing me. God had been there when my parents were incarcerated and my brother and I bounced from our grandmother's house into the care of an unfit foster parent. And He was there when I terminated my first pregnancy. He wept with me during my father's death. And He was grieved at the hurt Kyle and I experienced in our immature marriage. God was there with Sam and me, too. He smiled at our delight at one another and cautioned us when we moved too quickly. His voice didn't silence when I prayed for understanding as to why I kept losing people I loved. But He didn't give me an answer to my question. In my short time learning of God, it was clear His answer was rarely direct. Not this God. He was a parable speaking, lesson teaching, character pruning God and I was up for my next study.

***

The train ride back from church to Maryland felt longer than normal. A broken heart makes the days drag by. I was staring out the window when the conductor called out the next stop. Humming over the sound of the conductor was another voice. "Go see your mother," God said. I dug my heels into the floor of the train thinking to myself that there was no way in hell I was going to see my mother. As the train pulled up to my station and I had convinced myself I was being paranoid or delusional from a lack of a full night's rest, the voice came back louder. "Go see your mother," God repeated. "And call Kyle," was added parenthetically so much so that I wasn't sure if it was a command or a suggestion.

Both instructions were absurd. The last conversation my mother and I had involved her telling me very frankly that she never wanted to speak to me again. My mother was an intelligently calculated woman who was aware of the gravity of her words. When she told that she was done with me I took that as Gospel and resolved to make peace with the end of our relationship. My aspirations of being best friends with my mother were written off as another intangible. I also wasn't willing to test the limits of her boundaries because nothing frightened me more than my mother's anger. There was no telling how she would react to me showing up at her door unannounced and unwelcomed. God seemed to be putting me in a precarious predicament and I didn't like it one bit. But, I considered that He was all-knowing and that if He was instructing me to see my mother it must have meant something may have happened.

I pivoted in the direction of my mother's house, using the long walk to think about what I would say when I arrived. Inconveniently, God gave me instructions with no talking points for how this was to play out. I wasn't sure if I should lead with asking how she's been doing or if I needed to address the last argument we had. I was saddened by the state of our relationship and for the first time in the two years since we last spoke, I had a moment to truly consider the implications of a life without her. Our relationship was never strong; life hadn't given us a good start at developing a bond. I do remember some of my favorite moments with my mother being in the kitchen. As I passed the houses in her suburban neighborhood nostalgia gifted me with the smell of my mother's cooking.

My mother never said I love you, but she demonstrated her affection through home-cooked meals. Curry goat could be a reward for a job well done in school, and oxtail with rice and peas were household favorites when my mother was in a good mood. The best moments were when she let me sit in the kitchen to cook with her. Those were our rare opportunities to have conversations, and they were the few occasions I saw my mother at peace. My mother in the kitchen is the woman I longed to have at my side when I was going through my divorce and when Sam told me he wanted to break things off.

The front lawn was still shabby with patches where the family dog ironically named Patches had marked her territory. I looked for any sign of the house changing since my exodus. The second-floor shutters hinged out of place. And the screen door was still broken. In two years so much had happened in my life: a divorce, a new love, a broken heart. Most of all I was a Christian. My soul had been saved and my life was now marked with the promise of redemption. I wondered if my mother would grant me the same grace. Before knocking on the door I paused to see if God would gift me with precise instruction on what exactly I was supposed to do when in the presence of the woman who instructed me to disappear from her life. Pinch-hitting moments weren't high points of communication for God and me. Whether His inconvenient silence was intentional was yet to be understood, whatever the case I hoped for a sign, an edict.

Hell, a one-word command would have sufficed.

When it became clear God had either placed me on some kind of hold on a spiritual call or was testing my obedience, I gave the crackly front door a soft knock. I knew it wasn't loud enough for any capable person to hear. A minute passed before I gave the door one gentler tap. Just as I turned my back to leave my youngest sister peeked through the glass frame.

"Kirah?" I heard her say through the door. There was no turning back now.

"Hey Akeelah, is mommy home?"

"Yeah, she's upstairs," she said while letting me into the house.

My heart thumped to the pace of each step I took towards my mother's bedroom. Dryness cracked my tongue, which was going to make it difficult for me to talk. I was still collecting my thoughts. I had no idea why God led me to the home I escaped from on that particular day. Why had He ordered me to go back two years later?

The door of her bedroom was ajar and I could see my mother lying in the position she always oriented herself. She angled her body to the side so she could see the television while keeping close watch of trespassers of her private domain. Last I heard of my mother her fiancé had been dishonest about his friendships with other women, subsequently leading to the ending of their pending marriage. While I didn't care to involve myself in the details of my mother's love life it pained me to know she was facing another heartache. Having experienced two back-to-back heartbreaks of my own, I empathized with her pain. I stood at the door for a moment wondering if all the years of single parenting children pushed my mother into her bed day after day. There was a constant fatigue that hung over my mother. Her exasperation accompanied her in conversations with us, to her job, and there in the bed where she tried to bargain for some peace.

The door made a creaking noise as I pushed it open to make my way inside. My entrance into her bedroom was no less dangerous than entering a sleeping lion's den and I was no less certain I wasn't going to make it out alive.

"Who's there?" My mother asked. She pulled herself upright, using her hands to bench-press her body weight upward.

"It's me Shakirah, mommy," I said trying my hardest to sound unthreatening. She sat silently for a moment, glancing at me with the same confidence of someone who had been in on a secret. In the silence, I felt a nudge that pushed me around the frame of my mother's bed and into her arms. Then without any inhibition at all, the words and tears came flowing from me.

"I'm so sorry mommy. I'm sorry for everything." I cried as she cradled me in her chest.

"Oh, honey why are you crying?" She asked.

"Because I made you mad and I just disappeared."

"Sweetie, it's okay. A mother never stops praying for her child. I knew you would come back."

Now—when God told me to go see my mother the last scenario I played in my mind was one of me apologizing. It wasn't me who had ordered a moratorium on our relationship. And my ceasing to talk to her was in direct obedience to her request for us to never speak again. Yet, when my mother glanced in my direction when I announced myself at her bedroom door I could see a woman who, with all the perceptiveness of prophet, knew about the years of resentment her daughter harbored towards her. Yes, my mother had done and said many hurtful things to me growing up. Many of those things could rightfully be considered unforgivable. But, I hadn't permitted her to be human. I expected her to take the unfair hand life had dealt her and play a flawless game. I was unfair to my mother and for that, I needed her forgiveness.

Things were definitely still the same in that old household, including my mother's routine. After we rid ourselves of the remnants from sobbing my mother ordered me to retreat with her to the kitchen. A few years before I was seated on the counter announcing my engagement while my mother made curry chicken. I was a different woman then. My heart was burned with the ugliness of my past. As my mother pulled out all her ingredients I thought about telling her about Sam, but I decided otherwise.

My mother washed her vegetables with diligence and followed up by chopping them rhythmically. I imagined her being as graceful in the kitchen as she had been as a dancer. My mother's cooking was a performance: A dash of pepper here with a sprinkle of salt there. Boiling water and the crackling of oil in the Dutch pan added a beat to the backdrop of her movement. In moments the smell of seared meat permeated the kitchen. She whisked around grabbing pots, utensils, and ingredients without so much as letting anything overcook, even in the slightest. As she moved between the cabinets, stove, and fridge I remembered our times in the kitchen as a young girl. Her stories of growing up in England came back to me. I asked her to tell those stories again. I wanted to hear them with fresh ears and an open heart. I wanted to get to know this woman who cared enough to tell me she loved me by making my favorite meals.

***

I can't say I walked away from our reuniting with the assurance that we were going to have a strong relationship. Fear convinced me things we would go back to the way they had always been. We would spend time being cordial and then my mother would find a way to back me into a corner of child guilt. I wanted to remain on defense but God told me this time around I needed to go all in. And even if there remained the woman I grew to know as a child, I was still called to be different. God wanted me to be as consistent in my mother's life as He had been in mine. He wanted me to hold the line even if I was hurt. It was going to be the only way I could learn to push through the pain of my past.

It was never like my mother and me to talk every day so after a week of me calling her consistently, I was emotionally taxed. Our conversations never bore anything heavy. I asked about her day and she asked about mine. But, I felt out of place like I was trying to build a life with a stranger. For the first time, it was pristinely clear to me that I had no clue who my mother was outside of her role as a parent. It was also clear that I was going to have to lay down my expectations of what it meant for her to be a mother. All my life I wanted a mother—my mother—to validate my existence and when she couldn't do that I found my own means of validation. I also wanted my mother to acknowledge how much she hurt me. Time would reveal that her wants were different. My mother wanted to be seen as a woman whose heart was broken and desires were perpetually left unfilled. All her life she hung in the shadows of men unworthy of her heart and children she found it difficult to relate to. Going all in as God directed would mean me seeing her, truly seeing my mother as a woman.

My mother was born in a small town located in Kingston, Jamaica, to two entrepreneurs. Her mother, a brash yet remarkably brilliant woman, owned a number of restaurants and nightclubs throughout South London. And her father was a businessman with a proclivity to gambling and the bottle. His alcoholism led him to abandon my mother when she was just a little girl. When she reached primary school age my mother moved with her mother to England where she would attend boarding schools to become versed in the Classics and become a trained ballerina. Story has it that my mother was the first black woman to attend her boarding school, among many noble firsts, which included becoming an equestrian. As she grew in grace and stature her peers affectionately named her Patsy as a nod to her inherent poise.

But as sweet as she was, she was a small young woman with quick wit and an even quicker tongue. Patsy and her mother didn't get along and the absence of Patsy' father—who was said to have gambled the family's money away—left her feeling alone. So, she moved to America with the dream of becoming a dancer, making it her first point to gain acceptance in the prestigious Julliard School of Performing Arts. Patsy' plans were destroyed when she became pregnant at 17. And then again a few years later. And again. And again. By the time I arrived my mother had already had four children and her dreams were suppressed memories of what was supposed to be.

Eight children and countless heartbreaks erased any traces of Patsy. My mother as I knew her was a woman working two—sometimes—three jobs to keep the roof over our heads. And perhaps in the midst of negotiating how to reconcile her personal afflictions with the reality of what had become her life, she was too busy to see the cycle that had begun with my grandmother, was now living on through her.

Rarely did Patsy talk about Maddie, her mother. And when she did, there was always a tone of regret that hung in the backdrop of the conversation. What I gathered from the times Maddie entered our lives—like when she decided to be a temporary caregiver in my parents' absence—was that there had always been friction in their relationship. Maddie raised my oldest sister in hopes my mother would be able to redeem her aspirations and still pursue dancing. When my mother got pregnant again, the wedge that already existed between them, widened.

During Patsy's moments of rage, she would tell my siblings and me that we were lucky because her mother was a much harsher disciplinarian. According to my mother, whose words could be as scathing as a razor scrapped on the back of your knuckles, Maddie would throw blunt objects at my mother's head or beat her mercilessly if she so much as appeared to be stepping out of line. As I got to know my mother I started to see that she had only been giving me what she was exposed to.

In her life, there had never been real demonstrations of love. Maddie, her father, and all the men who abandoned her with small children at her side eroded any beliefs she could have unconditional love. To expect my mother to operate out of any place greater than her own experiences was unfair. Some are able to give the love they have never received and that is a remarkable feat. For most, however, when no love has been imparted—as was the case with my mother—then the individual responds from the void of that love.

Our conversations became less awkward with time; I developed the comfort and security to share things that were happening in my life. I started by telling her how I had taken up running, which came to her surprise since we were a family of dancers, writers, and all-around artsy folks. I talked about the pain of losing Sam.

"Oh, honey—" she said as I laid on the edge of her bed.

"If it's right it will come back to you." I didn't know how my mother could retain that level of optimism given all she experienced. But I started to see things in her that I admired like her wisdom and her cunning ability to balance enough sass to keep you on your toes with an intellect that made you want to engage her more.

My Sundays were once occupied by afternoon walks or evening dinners with Sam. Now I was spending them at my mother's side cooking, watching her favorite British shows and gossiping about celebrities we would never know or meet. I watched as my mother became impassioned when talking about local politics. She lauded at America *finally* having a black president. Then she could, without missing a date, recall any fact of ancient history as if it happened yesterday. This woman who I had spent years despising was cool and beautiful and brilliant and funny. The more time we shared the more I realized how alike we were. We weren't only mother and daughter; we were two women who wanted many of the same things from life. The most prominent of those things was to be loved.

***

The seasons were changing in more ways than one. My life was becoming something different, new. Internally, I could feel a shift in my response to life's circumstances. I missed Sam but I also understood the necessity in our break up. At the time of our courtship I was not a healthy person and though I had made the decision to surrender my life to God, the process of healing had not been completed in me. Unfinished business in my life needed attending to that had to occur without the validation of a man—no matter how wonderful that man was to me. I needed to get to know this new Shakirah that God brought into the world.

I shared my spiritual journey with my mother while bringing over my furniture for her to have.

"I can't understand why you're getting rid of this perfectly good living room set." She said as I gave suggestions on where she should place the cushioned ottoman I had grown to love.

"God told me to get rid of everything," I responded.

It was true. God did tell me to leave all of my furniture behind. The condo Kyle and I purchase was up for sale and I was praying about moving back to New York. Our home and everything in it was the remaining fragment of the life we shared. My mother didn't respond when I shared what I believed God said. I could tell she was happy to be on the receiving end of my obedience.

The transformation occurring in my heart made me hopeful God could do the same in my mother. When I was a young girl and woman I wanted her to change so that her behavior could benefit me. My thinking was that if she had been a kinder mother, my life would have been easier. God's love for me changed my perspective. I wanted my mother to experience the healing I was undergoing for herself. I wanted her to know the peace and joy. My prayers started to include my mother: that she would know God deeply, and in time find someone to truly love her.

On holidays I invited her to attend Holy Gates with me. Because my mother worked two jobs it was difficult for her to make the time. I also think she wasn't ready to take on that level of spiritual commitment. Patsy abandoned her Catholic upbringing when she married my father who was a Rastafarian. She spoke of God abstractly in the same manner a person speaks of someone they've seen in passing but doesn't know intimately. She never denied the existence of God, but she never acted on any belief she may have had.

After years of not seeing Patsy on Mother's Day, she accompanied me to Holy Gates' Mother's Day service. When we walked into the theater I felt proud to introduce Patsy to my church friends. I don't know if others around us could feel the power of the moment, but I could sense God's presence. The power of His grace had gifted Patsy and me with reconciliation. I never imagined I could be happy with my mother standing by my side as I worshipped God. I was a proud daughter. Like Christ had forgiven the debt of my sins I had let go of my mother's mistakes. It was enough to have her there, present, with me. We were getting a chance to start over and I wanted to do it with a clean slate.

During Mother's Day brunch at a boutique French restaurant in DC's Eastern Market, I asked Patsy about Maddie. I knew that talking about her mother was a sensitive subject since Maddie's death but I wanted to understand their history more so that we could make sure we didn't repeat it. The restaurant was filled with families showering their respective matriarchs in love. Patsy and I sat at a corner table adjacent to the restaurant's largest window where the sun was boasting. I ordered two mimosas in celebration of my mother and to lighten the mood around the conversation.

"I never got a chance to forgive my mother," Patsy said as she took the first sip of her drink.

Her West Indian, British and downtown New York accents blended when she tried to hide emotion. And her voice always cracked when she spoke of Maddie. My grandmother died a few months after my father's murder. My depression and grieving blinded me from seeing how both of their deaths impacted my mother. Whatever grief she experienced she hid behind a rock-like exterior. Patsy made funeral and flight arrangements without shedding a tear. Whatever pain she had been holding to then she was finally letting out.

"—She wasn't always the easiest person to get along with but she was still my mother and I wish we could've gotten past our differences."

It was rare to see my mother vulnerable. As she talked about her regrets her body appeared much smaller. The edges around her that always struck me as rough were softening.

"Do you miss her?" I asked naively.

"No, I don't miss her. Just wish things could've been different."

"Listen—" she said as she changed the conversation.

"I know I have made mistakes but I want you to know I always tried for you. I had to work and fight to keep a roof over our heads and the lights on. It wasn't always enough, I know that, but it was the best I could give."

I sat listening not wanting to break the moment. Normally, this level of intimacy would have made me uncomfortable but I knew God had led me to my mother's door for a reason and months later that reason was becoming clear.

"My decisions for you weren't always popular but I made them because I wanted you to have the life I couldn't live. I didn't want you saddled down with a bunch of babies like me. All any parent wants for their children is for them to live a better life than we have."

Patsy wasn't apologizing, not in the way I had daydreamed an apology would occur. But for my sake and for hers I gave the one thing we both desperately needed to set us free— forgiveness.

***

Chapter Eleven

A New Hope

The years following my divorce from Kyle and subsequent break up with Sam moved quickly. It was as if the hurt I experienced from those losses was a recurring bad dream. I knew the pain I endured was real but the aching was more distant than it had been before. The sense of time passing hadn't removed me from the aching. I outgrew the way I allowed the pain to impact me. Instead of seeing my traumas and heartaches as kinks in my armor, I saw them as lessons.

When I was faced with the decision to abort my first pregnancy; my father's murder, the breakdown of my relationship with my mother, the dissolution of my first marriage and walking away from what looked like promising love, it would appear as though I had been collecting lessons. Lessons that made me humble and gentle. Lessons that gave me incredible compassion for anyone who was walking with an emotional limp. Lessons that continued to remind me of God who never left me to face these challenges on my own.

Lessons that would be guideposts for walking into a new life and a new hope. The pain was benevolent in that way. My momentary sorrow hadn't been in vain.

Life looked much different than five years prior. After spending months crashing on friends' couches and deciding where I wanted to plant my feet, I landed in the heart of DC in a one bedroom sublet condo. The move was unexpected because I spent so much time contemplating and planning a move back to New York to set out on my dream of being a writer in the big city. I pictured myself in my hometown of Brooklyn walking through Flatbush with a journal in one hand and a coffee in the other. I smiled at the thought of me walking with such self-assurance. I smiled at the realization that I didn't put Sam or Kyle — not even Patsy —at the center of my motivations.

I wanted to be back in New York yet something felt unfinished in DC. I had a sense that my story was at the precipice of restarting but I would have to close out a chapter. I followed that belief of needing to finish out what I perceived as an incomplete chapter when I signed the lease on the home, where I completed the first few drafts of this book. My new condo was a conservative space that hooked me with a den I fashioned into a writing room. For the first time in my life, I had a physical and mental space of my own.

***

The year of my 30th birthday, Spring emerged in DC with the same gentleness of a doe that walks up on the creek to get a sip of water. The evening rush halted to a calm making the city quiet. I developed a new hobby of getting lost in the side streets of my neighborhood. Walking to my favorite coffee bar for a writing session I could see families gather around dining room tables in rowhomes that border the area's restaurants and coffee shops. I thought about what it might be like to have a family of my own and I sometimes wondered how my life would have looked if Sam and I pushed through my brokenness. Would I have been a mother by now? Would we be one of those families squeezing and kissing our juicy brown babies as we gathered around the dinner table for a meal?

The sun was making its last appearance for the day when the fireflies began dancing and lighting up the night. On that walk, I resolved that Sam and I weren't intended to go the distance. He did, however, show me that love could be possible when the timing was right. Sam also showed me that I was deserving of a partner who would be willing to build a relationship based on authenticity, love, trust, and reciprocity.

In this way, Kyle and Sam were the polarities of my experiences. In Kyle, I saw the worst parts of myself. Being married to Kyle, the darkest part of my heart was nurtured through self-pity and rage. If I didn't emerge out of being a victim, I would continue to be with more Kyles. Sam was the opposite. Though we entered into a relationship before I was ready to be involved with someone new, he opened my mind to a new kind of love. I loved Kyle and Sam equally yet differently. I could never undermine my relationship with Kyle simply because we both married the wrong person, just as I couldn't overestimate that Sam was going to be the answer to my problems. They were two paths I chose to walk, and I'm glad I walked them both.

***

I dated a bit while I was emerging into my new space as a young woman. I found myself getting smarter about the men I allowed in my proximity and with each prospect that didn't manifest into something more, I made note of what I liked about me when I was with these men. I knew of what I desired in a romantic partner. Dating was teaching me about what I desired to be. It didn't take much time before I realized I would need to continue to be alone for a bit longer. After several rounds of opening myself up to the possibility of partnering with someone and being mildly disappointed by the revelation that I need to mature a bit more before going the distance, I vowed to be single. I went on a dating and relationships fast that would end only when I knew the time was right.

It was a scary thought to crouch on the doorstep of turning 30 and decide that was the moment I wanted to be alone especially when everyone around me was getting married and starting families. I evaded the fear and pressed forward in my solitude. While everyone was finding romantic love, I was finding love in my own words and my own voice. My essays were getting published in prominent publications like RELEVANT Magazine, one of the largest contemporary magazines for Christians and *Vanity Fair*. I had something of a blossoming career, too. Without the weight of distractions, I found that I was an incredibly talented businesswoman and marketer.

More than an enriching career, I was seeing my friendships and the relationship with my mother in a new light. My friends stood with me through my divorce and they remained in my corner with every decision I made thereafter. Showing up for them as they stepped out on their own paths was an honor.

Noori and Jackson allowed me to share in their joy when they had their first child, a baby girl with a head full of bouncy curls. Each of the women in the Chocolate Suite was forging into new directions. One started her own business, an event planning company. One of my friends and her long-term partner got engaged. I was there for it all and when I couldn't physically be there, I was with them carried in their hearts because of the depth of our bond.

Patsy and I took the slow and steady road toward reconciliation. We were perceptive in realizing that we were two women whose lives were connected through DNA, yes, but whose stories were not fully understood and embraced. I wanted to use this time to get to know my mother. We called each other regularly and the more we talked the more it felt like I was gaining a new friend rather than a mother.

There were times when I remained reluctant to be fully vulnerable with Patsy. I was apprehensive to share too much information about myself out of fear that somehow Patsy would throw it in my face. I was ashamed of my feelings because I could tell that my mother was trying. Patsy was opening herself up just as I was doing. She was being vulnerable. The revelation of her vulnerability came to me on the day when my mom had told me she met someone new. Like me, Patsy was perpetually single. Unlike me, she was on a mission to end her single streak. We were on the phone when she called to share the news.

"I like him a lot but I don't know, baby. I'm scared."

It was the first time I heard Patsy tell me she was scared and I loved her all the more for being so open with me. Together, we talked through the fear of starting over. We took turns commiserating on how hard it was to hold onto the belief on an everlasting and enduring love.

On a Saturday night, Patsy had come to my place to help me clean out my closet, which was more of her taking everything I was no longer wearing and claiming it for herself.

"You've always had a good eye for style," Patsy said while picking up dresses as I tossed them to the ground.

"You get that from me, you know? I was the one who

taught your father how to dress."

In our new relationship, Patsy wasn't afraid to talk about things that were previously unspoken. When she spoke of Winston, she did so lovingly and with the witty humor, I had only seen glimpses of in my childhood.

In between taking and tossing articles of clothing, Patsy continued her line of questioning until we landed on the topic of dating.

"Are you seeing anyone?" she asked.

"No, I'm really just focused on my career right now. There's always going to be time to date."

"Honey — careers come and go. Don't put your love life on the backburner."

"And love will always be there, too. Right?" I continued on with my closet clearing.

"You had a career and eight kids. You didn't let a man stop you."

"I had eight kids and it was hard. I had to work those jobs. I had to fight to keep food on our table and it I wish I didn't have to work so hard. I wish I could have slowed down a little."

"Can I ask you a question — did you want to be a mother?"

"No woman who doesn't want to be a mother has eight kids, Shakirah. Of course, I wanted to be a mother. I didn't always get it right but I love my children — every single one of you. Look, I know that divorce rocked you. I see how badly it shook you up, but you can't hide behind ambition. You have to allow yourself to believe in love again. I admire that you want to be a Renaissance woman. I just want you to learn from me. Slow down a bit. Let the love come. You're my daughter. You deserve it."

My birthday was weeks away and my mother had already

given me the best gift. Her words were encouraging. She gave me the reassurance that I mattered to her and even when I didn't think she knew who I was as a person, she knew me at my core. My mother knew my soul because we once shared it.

***

My spiritual journey had evolved like everything else in my life. I remained a member of Holy Gates Church and actively participated in growing the church. I also saw how important it was for me to remain connected to my faith through a relationship with God. I continued my practice of prayer, learning how to pray in new ways like through writing and running.

On my runs, I became reflective on the years of my spiritual journey and the ways I might summarize how I entered into the kingdom of God. It started as a decision I made in my heart. Then it moved to something greater — a deep sacrifice of letting go of everything I knew and believed before to grasp onto a life I wouldn't have been able to draw if I had been given the option.

Surrender was my launch pad. What occurred after I made the decision to let go was up to God. From where I was sitting at that time in my life, the decision didn't always appear well worth the investment. When I decided to set my emotional brokenness and baggage before God it never occurred to me that my life could get any worse. Divorce, giving up my first home, another fall out with my mother and heartbreak all came after I offered my heart to God. What I couldn't see then was that the cataclysmic series of events were necessary parts of the journey. As Pastor Rubio often said, death must always precede resurrection.

The challenges in my life had not been passed on to me

without the permission of the Creator insomuch as when the old me died, spiritually, the life I knew before was also dying. An aborted baby; my father's murder; the marriage I shouldn't have been in; the condo that shouldn't have been purchased; the dysfunctional relationship with my mother; the loss of a new love. All death. But a life filled with freedom was on the horizon.

***

Friends had come from all over as I celebrated my 30th birthday. We spent the night gathered in a trendy new Italian restaurant downtown. I was filled with gratitude for the occasion and for the way life was aligning. I was in a new city, entering a new decade with a new perspective. I was an actualized woman with new goals and dreams. Maybe love would come. Maybe it wouldn't. Maybe I would have my chance at motherhood. Maybe I wouldn't. I didn't have a clear plan or feel the pressure to create one. I wanted to take my mother's advice and let everything that was intended for me to come. I didn't have to push or force the plans for my life to happen. They would unfold as they were intended to. God didn't need my help in manifesting the days of my life. He only needed me to stay surrendered.

With the start of the new year of life, I found a rhythm I didn't have before. I went to work. I came home. I chatted with my friends. It was all so normal. But for me everything as a freedwoman was marvelous. A life that I didn't have to live in constant fear or anxiety was novel. I sat in wonder after work, taking in the quiet, letting peace swell in my heart.

***

"Thank you, God," I would say over and over again.

Like every Sunday morning, I woke to prepare myself for church service. I ran to the catch the bus going headed toward Chinatown. On my ride, I read through some scriptures landing on one that had given my heart comfort when it was in the middle of aching. "For I know the plans I have for you declares the Lord, plans to prosper you and not harm you. Plans for hope and a future." Plans for hope and future I said to myself before looking out the window. Everything was as it should be.

I always liked that on Sunday mornings the city would still be asleep after the Saturday night rumble and tumble. I hopped off the bus and walked towards the theater. In the distance, I thought I spotted a recognizable figure but brushed it off. I knew service would be starting soon so I forced my stride to move quicker. As I picked up my pace the indiscernible figure became clearer. I knew that walk. I could spot that frame from anywhere. By now I was jogging forward to see if my mind had been playing tricks on me. The person ahead of me moved with ease unaware that I was coming closer.

I entered the theater and climbed onto the escalator losing the person who had been in front of me. As the escalator drew closer to the top level I spotted him again. From that distance he was unmistakable. The tall, basketball-player physique only belonged to one person. The escalator arrived at the top where our eyes met. Without thinking I walked into his arms to give him a welcoming hug.

"How ya doin'?" He asked, his Midwestern twang once again humming in my ear.

"I'm great, Sam. I'm really great." I said as I let go.

And for once it was true because I was finally free.

***

A New Hope

Acknowledgements

Writing this book has been one of the most rigorous and rewarding experiences of my life. There are many people whose encouragement, support and care made completing *Until My Surrender* possible.

I would like to start by thanking my family for trusting me to tell pieces of our collective story through my lens. Thank you for keeping me grounded and for showing me that imperfection in a family can be quite beautiful.

To my intelligent, beautiful and formidable mother, I'm grateful for the sacrifices you've made so that I could live out my dreams. Your strength has been a pillar in my life even when I didn't want to acknowledge it.

Rashidi, my big brother, and first best friend, you've always believed in me. I'm proud to be your baby sister.

Ayanna, my sister-cousin, your mentorship, and example have helped me mature into a woman who now knows how to unapologetically advocate for herself.

To Bako, Candyce, Latoya, Patrice and Teresa, thank you for teaching me another dimension of love and commitment. Your friendship carried me through one of my darkest periods. It is an honor to have dedicated this book to you.

Itunu, thank you for following the Spirit's leading and supporting me as I transitioned from one season to another.

Danielle and Jenna, you've both shown me, in different ways, that having it all is possible. Thank you for gifting me with my godchildren, the most perfect human beings. Every FaceTime, video message, picture and phone call sustained me on the days that were hard to push through.

I would also like to thank my spiritual family at GCC. Thank you to the pastors for your leadership and guidance. Thank you for caring for me when I was just a baby Christian learning to navigate my faith. Thank you to everyone who prayed for and with me throughout this process.

Afa and Vanessa my writing partners, thank you for keeping me accountable. Thank you for pushing me to finish what I started.

I would be remiss not to thank my editor Ali Lawrence, the Book Doula. Ali, it is because of you I was able to get this book over the finish line. Thank you for helping me find my confidence as an author. Jerome, you stepped out of your comfort zone to design a book cover that thoughtfully and poetically captures the heart of my story. I'm so grateful to have your creative, Midas touch be apart of this project. Thank you to Debra, my brand manager, and assistant, for keeping me organized and focused.

Finally, I would like to thank my best friend and future husband, Matthew. It is said that anyone pursuing a purpose should remember their why. You are my reason. You are my why.

And to everyone who has purchased, read and shared this book I remain indebted to you for joining in my story. Thank you for making my dreams come true.

About the Author

Growing up amid challenging circumstances, Shakirah Hill learned to use writing and speaking as tools to advocate for teen girls and women so that they might find emotional wellness and freedom. By telling the story of her faith in Jesus, Shakirah works to catalyze a generation of women to live the abundant life they are promised.

As a writer, Shakirah focuses on the intersectionality of media, race, gender and faith. Her work has been featured in publications such as RELEVANT Magazine, Off the Page, Teen Vogue, and Vanity Fair. Shakirah's speaking platform covers overcoming brokenness, self-confidence development, and spiritual growth. Some of her speaking clients include the Girl Scouts of America, Sharon Bible Fellowship Church, the Public Relations Society of America, Creative Mornings DC, and Ladies America.

In addition to writing and speaking Shakirah works full-time as the Vice President of Digital Strategy for Metropolitan Group, a creative services agency focused on social impact.

Shakirah is an active member of her community church. In her spare time, Shakirah volunteers as a mentor with Horton's Kids. She is also an avid runner, enjoys cooking, and traveling. Shakirah earned her B.A. in English and Literature with a minor in Art History from the University of Maryland at College Park where she graduated with honors. She graduated cum laude from Georgetown University where she holds a master's degree in Integrated Marketing.

Shakirah currently resides in Washington, DC. Her debut

memoir Until My Surrender: A Story of Loss, Love and Letting Go will be available fall 2018.

Shakirah can be reached at www.shakirahadianna.com

CPSIA information can be obtained
at www.ICGtesting.com
Printed in the USA
FFHW011712041218
49753768-54216FF